'If you are new as a leader-manager read and learn.
If you are an experience leader-manager read on.'

Wendy Hughes, Head of Learning and Development, BAM Nuttall Ltd

Bei_____ile
Leader-Manager

Practical skills to handle people challenges in today's world of work

Catherine Joyce

Being An Agile Leader-Manager

First published in 2016 by

Panoma Press Ltd
48 St Vincent Drive, St Albans, Herts, AL1 5SJ, UK
info@panomapress.com
www.panomapress.com

Book design and layout by Neil Coe.

Printed on acid-free paper from managed forests.

ISBN 978-1-784520-79-3

Dedication

To David

without whom this and much else would not have been possible.

Authorised Testimonials

I was thrilled when Catherine asked me to read her book. I expected it to be insightful, full of her words of wisdom and presented in an easy-to-read format. I wasn't disappointed. This will sit in my bookcase alongside the greats as a tool for reference when I'm working through an approach or when I'm designing leader-manager learning interventions. It's full of useful exercises, rich in short, thought-provoking statements, truly helpful relatable case stories and years of experience in many different sectors of work. Well done Catherine. This is a great read. I really enjoyed it.

If you are new as a leader-manager read and learn. If you are an experienced leader-manager read on, there are new things to learn and some things to refresh thinking on. This spans the years of leader-manager practice.

**Wendy Hughes,
Head of Learning and Development, BAM Nuttall Ltd**

Read it! This is one of the most engaging, real-world management books I've read in a long time. It was like getting a shot of Catherine. You were here with me, being highly engaging, fun, businesslike and motivational.

**James Roseblade,
General Manager, Jemca Lexus**

Catherine is an inspirational exec coach and brilliant facilitator at getting 'You' to get the best out of 'You'. Through her teachings, guidance and support I continue to grow each day as an effective Leader. 'Being an Agile Leader-Manager – practical skills to handle people challenges, in today's world of work' is an essential part of the current or aspiring leader-manager's toolbox; I'd challenge anyone using the book not to identify, learn and improve with it.

**John Slaven,
Engineering Manager, Bam Nuttall**

Catherine's book is excellent. It really explains the key things that a leader-manager needs to handle effectively in today's complex organisational environment to deliver success. It's an excellent 'go to' resource for any manager who wants to be successful at managing people. This book gets to the real essence and issues that confront leader-managers in the complex world of business today, providing a valuable guide to the challenges they face.

**Andrew Exon,
Group Operations Director, John Roe Toyota Group**

I've read some 'Management' books before and they have been a trudge with no real learning at the end other than a whole load of terms I'll never use.

This book has substance and meaning. The stories and exercises and '?' sections allow/invite the reader to 'do' something rather than being passive.

**Chris Smith,
Director of Training**

How very grateful would I have been earlier in my career if a manager or mentor had handed me your book. It is brilliantly segmented and specific in areas of focus. It works on every level and it would inspire any manager/ leader in my industry to action. I actively recommend it to current and aspiring managers – and to organisations who wish to turn their technical talent into the leaders of the future.

**Keith J Barnard
MIMI, I.Eng, MSOE, MIRTE, TPS
Manager at VW Group**

Acknowledgments

To my daughter Ellen – blossoming beautifully; you are an emerging leader with so much potential. Thank you for making me laugh when the going got tough while I was writing draft 2; and for reflecting back my own advice at me, in a way that only you can, my darling

To my son Ross, of whom I am so proud. You are already a leader in your own life and have much to contribute. You make me laugh like no one else.

Thanks to Wendy Hughes, who has been a collaborator, kindred spirit, as well as client for many happy and lovely years. Many tools and techniques in the book were practised and refined in the SLP and ELP programmes you commissioned.

Thank you to James Roseblade, Wendy Hughes, Andrew Exon and Keith Barnard for taking the time to read my manuscript in the raw state and who thankfully saw through the rawness; thank you for your kindness and encouraging words.

Special thanks go to John Slaven for the time and effort you put in, giving me valuable, detailed feedback and insights on the manuscript. Arran's name is mentioned, just where you added it.

Over the years I've learned with and from a myriad of exceptional consultants, managers, facilitators, coaches and friends who include Lee-Anne, Lucy, Jenny, Fiona, Maeve and all the gang I worked with in Optima; the inspirational Dr Mel Parr in PIPPIN; Sarah Sweetman and Dorothea Tsoflias in Organisational Edge.

Throughout my working life I've been blessed to meet people who have opened up ways for me to contribute. Those that come to mind, in addition to those mentioned above include Ian D Williams, Dr Mel Parr, David Lewis, Simon Boxall, Steve Fox and Garry Crabtree, Helen Walpole, Jorgen Blum, Mike Worthington, John Brett. Thank you all.

To Nick Heap, Colin Hill and Jean Woolward – all wise and inspirational friends over many years.

Thanks to Mindy, my Book Midwife, Emma, Alison and all the team who have helped me give birth to my book.

And finally, an especially big 'thank you' to the hundreds of leader-managers, clients, teams and groups that I have facilitated or coached over the years. It's been my honour to work with you. I have been inspired by you too, learned from you and laughed with you. I hope some of you will recognise yourselves in the stories throughout the book (names changed to protect the innocent!).

May you all continue to flourish.

Contents

Chapter 6: Managing Good Performance and Underperformance 137

Chapter 7: How to Be an Effective Leader-Manager 171

Introduction

Leader-managers are among the group of people I most admire in the world. That's why I love working with them. Many become leaders and managers by accident more than design and yet they take on the mantle of responsibility and do their very best to get it right.

Sometimes they find themselves facing situations they are just not trained to handle. Often they are promoted into leadership and management roles because they are so competent at something else, such as sales, engineering, marketing, finance, IT, etc.

For over 20 years I have worked in learning and development within – and also as an external consultant for – a number of well-known organisations, and my remit has predominantly been to help leader-managers develop the skills, confidence and competence to flourish.

Leadership development programmes are not only about learning skills they can bring back to the organisation. I believe they start with the individual. As Michael Neill calls it in his book *The Inside-Out Revolution,* it's all about leading from the inside out. Those I work with find themselves taking a good look in the mirror in order to identify and recognise not only where their strengths lie, but also where they need to learn new approaches and techniques; where to shape up or sharpen up.

> Being agile as a leader-manager can bring you great success.

The challenge for managers and leaders is to deliver success in today's complex organisational environment; and it has never been more challenging and exciting to be a 'people manager'. The need for 'agility' in how employees are led and managed has never been as relevant as it is today.

Yet, it is not without its challenges. That's why I've written this book. Today, much is expected of people managers in the workplace. Some deliver what is expected; many fail. There is a need for people managers to fully understand not only the landscape in which they are managing and working, but also the technicalities of people management.

The key to success in business is the ability to manage your team successfully. However, with the ever-changing makeup of teams and organisational structures, it is more challenging to deliver to the organisation and to the individual.

This is why you must be agile if you wish to be successful. You must learn ways and approaches that make you agile.

> The challenge for managers is to
> deliver success in today's complex
> organisational environment.

Downsizing through re-organisations, efficiency drives, buy-outs, mergers and acquisitions and the recent global recession have changed the workplace landscape forever.

Today's high-speed workplace organisations comprise full-time, part-time and zero-hour contracts, virtual teams and geographically spread teams, many of whom frequently communicate virtually rather than face to face. Joint venture partnership working is now commonplace in some industries, while communicating via social media and online tools are so prevalent they have changed how work gets done. Being managed in the 'old way' doesn't work in this new environment.

> There is a need for 'people managers' to fully
> understand not just the landscape in which
> they are managing and working, but also the
> technicalities of people management.

As a leader-manager, you will be aware that technology offers methodologies for efficiency, engagement, involvement, planning and organisation, time management, fitness and many more. Yet for organisations to succeed, people need more than efficient systems and processes. They need effective leadership and management.

To achieve success today requires a flexible,
adept leader-manager approach.

The greatest naivety a manager can exhibit
is to work on the assumption that effective
leadership and management skills will develop
without action, without effort.

In this book

In this book you will learn about the seven areas that will help set you apart as a leader-manager so that you can achieve the level of success you aspire to.

1. **Handling difficult conversations** is the number one activity that 95% of leader-managers I've worked with in recent years report that they struggle with. Why? Well, they're difficult. They often don't achieve the outcome you hoped for. People get defensive, become discouraged or disengaged and the conversation frequently meanders off course. Having the confidence to handle these conversations is essential if you want to build a platform for success.

We'll explore how you can prepare well and handle these conversations to much better effect.

2. We all know the saying 'practice makes perfect' but who has time for practice and repetition? Too few managers – and it gets them into all kinds of trouble. You want to be a good manager, right?

This is much more likely to happen when you understand that it takes **rehearsal, practice, repetition**, refinement to **'get it in the muscle'**. There is no silver bullet that will make you an effective leader-manager, but investing time and effort now will serve you forever.

3 and 4. To manage and lead people effectively (not only those who report to you, but peers, seniors, clients, suppliers, contractors, etc), it important to understand **how to communicate and manage expectations**; it's key to be able to set up accountabilities and hold people to them. Failure to anticipate and **deal with likely resistance** to new business opportunities, new ideas and change, will be the death knell for your organisation.

> There is no silver bullet that will make you an effective leader-manager.

5. **Managing performance** can be tricky. Years ago a 'command and control' culture existed where discipline and boundaries were strict and upheld. No longer. Today's employees want to be praised, engaged, motivated, well paid and given opportunities for promotion and development. This is essential to engender a 'feel good' environment.

At the same time, many in today's workforce are less open to being disciplined. Consequently, there's a tendency by managers to 'ignore it and it'll go away' or 'let's just hope it gets better all on its own' because 'I don't want to upset them'. Failing to **manage underperformance** hurts the performance of the business as well as being a poor message to send to customers, employees and contractors alike.

> These skills will set you apart as a leader-manager.

6. Added to the changes in workplace environment, we have the presence in the workplace of **three generations** at one time (for the first time in recent history). This presents leader-managers with challenges and opportunities that, if handled well, will impact the success of the organisation.

7. You'll learn that my take on this is that **who you are as a leader-manager**, your values, skills and confidence, all greatly influence the impact you have as you manage people around you.

It's true that having a few fundamental skills will help you get the best from this book and the tools you'll find here. For instance: skilled listening, flexible questioning, rapport building, everyday courage of your own convictions, calibrating others' behaviour, willingness to go through a 'trial and error' process in order to achieve a good level of competence and a decent level of self-awareness.

The purpose of all leader-managers is to drive the organisation forward and to achieve outstanding results. For this, today, you need agility. If your purpose in reading this book is to become more 'agile' as a leader-manager, I hope you will find that agility within.

In essence

- Everyone who manages people is a leader and a manager = leader-manager

- Success as a manager or leader today requires agility – of behaviour, mindset and attitude

- Leadership and management are learned skills; they don't come as standard in humans!

- To be effective as a leader-manager requires a good level of competence as a people manager

- Personality, inherent characteristics, values, as well as experience and skills, determine the kind of leader-manager you are

- There's never been a greater need in organisations for competent people management.

Sayings that this book encapsulates

Every man's conduct is an unspoken sermon that is forever preaching to others.
– Swiss philosopher Henri Amiel

The challenge of leadership is to be strong, but not rude; be kind, but not weak; be bold, but not a bully; be thoughtful, but not lazy; be humble, but not timid; be proud, but not arrogant; have humour, but without folly.
– Jim Rohn

Control is not leadership; management is not leadership; leadership is leadership. If you seek to lead, invest at least 50% of your time in leading yourself – your own purpose, ethics, principles, motivation, conduct. Invest at least 20% leading those with authority over you and 15% leading your peers.
– Dee Hock, Founder and CEO Emeritus, Visa

If you are persistent you will get it.
If you are consistent you will keep it.
– Unknown

I think that the best training a top manager can be engaged in is management by example. I want to make sure there is no discrepancy between what we say and what we do. I believe the best training is management by example. Don't believe what I say. Believe what I do.
– Carlos Ghosn, CEO of Renault-Nissan

Our chief want is someone who will inspire
us to be what we know we could be.
– Ralph Waldo Emerson

Before you are a leader, success is all about growing yourself.
When you become a leader, success is all about growing
others.
– Jack Welch

When you accept a leadership role, you take on extra
responsibility for your actions towards others.
– Kelly Armstrong

Remembering that I'll be dead soon is the most important tool
I've ever encountered to help me make the big choices in life.
Because almost everything – all external expectations, all pride,
all fear of embarrassment or failure – these things just fall away in
the face of death, leaving only what is truly important.
– Steve Jobs

People learn how to treat you based on
what you accept from them.
– Unknown

If your actions inspire others to dream more, learn more,
do more, and become more – you are a leader.
– John Quincy Adams

CHAPTER 1

The Three Generations at Work

You may notice as you read on that this chapter differs from the others as it explores the context/environment in which you, I and others are leading and managing today. By this I mean the societal, virtual, economic and political landscape that surrounds us in the 2010s.

The reason I begin with this chapter is that it forms the backdrop and landscape for the skills, techniques and approaches contained in this book.

Not only is the content of each chapter of practical use to leader-managers, these approaches have the potential to set you and your team up for success. These approaches are essential for delivering results through people. People, after all, are an organisation's greatest asset and organisations thrive or fail because of how the people in them are led and managed.

In this chapter we're going to:

- take a look at some of the statistics of our current workforce (in the UK) and compare and contrast some of the age profiles as they relate to the three generations

- see how having the three generations working together is a really good thing

- explore and help you understand the characteristics of each of the three generations at work

- find how best to manage each generation

- consider how to lead and manage them well and avoid trying to 'fix' them

The three generations that are the focus of this chapter are:

Baby Boomer – born 1946-1960
Generation X – born 1961-1980
Generation Y – born 1981-2000

(And I'll even say a little about Generation Z who have not yet entered the workplace in any numbers.)

Changing times

In many organisations today, if you take a look around you on an average working day, you won't be surprised to notice that there are people of all ages in the work environment.

They all bring their own attitudes, experiences and values to the workplace. Often the workplace is a melting pot like no other. This makes for a myriad of interesting, predictable and challenging interactions, some of which work and many which, unintentionally, undermine those involved.

Did you know there are more people over 65 years of age in the workforce than at any other time in history? This is partly because people are healthier and living longer; many don't want to retire right now as they have more to contribute; and yet others can't afford to give up work.

There's been much research on these different generations at work, much of it highlighting the differences between them – and some looking at what they share. Just do an internet search for 'the three generations at work' and you can browse for hours.

The concept is an interesting and pertinent one for managers, which is why I'm including it. Without exception, every leadership group I have discussed this with over the past six years or so has had very varied and stimulating conversations about the three generations. The topic generates a wide range of attitudes – from institutionalised age discrimination, intolerance and bias to respect, appreciation and excitement about the possibility of bridging the communication gap that is said to exist, in order to maximise the best of each for the benefit of the organisation as well as the team.

Whether or not you've come across the three generations at work before, read on. It can give you another perspective on what their needs may be, how you might wish to approach them or topics / issues relating to them and how to harness the differing motivations of the different groups. Of course, this will involve generalising, so please be aware of that as you read. At the same time, it's worth considering the insights in terms of how it can help you as a leader-manager to get the best from, and better engage and influence, each person – and how you can get the three generations working together and communicating more effectively.

What the three generations are and what makes them tick. We'll discover how each generation is defined and how they see themselves. Then, once you understand a bit about them and what makes them different from each other, you can plan how to work well with them and help them all work well together and prevent small differences becoming major challenges in the team and workplace.

How you can get the three generations
working together and communicating more
effectively.

You will be aware that over the past 75 years there have been massive changes to the society we live in. Take the first three series of *Downton Abbey*: set in an Edwardian country house at the turn of and into the 20th Century, *Downton Abbey* follows the lives, loves and relationships of the Crawley family and the servants who work for them. Across the three series everything changes and we see the birth, after World War II, of the first generation we'll explore in this book. They are called Baby Boomers (BBs).

> Why should employers care if employees
> in the different generations respect and
> understand each other? Three words:
> retention; productivity; sustainability.

The years for each generation vary from one historian, government agency and marketing firm to the next. For example, Neil Howe and the late William Strauss defined the Generation X generation in the broadest terms I have come across: 1961 to 1981. Yet others define it as being 1964 to 1979.

Bear in mind as you read on that since 'generations' are defined by generalised shared experiences, you may find that, depending on where you were born, what country you grew up in and the socio/political/familial influences that surrounded you, you may identify with one generation more than another – and that elements of more than one generation may also resonate.

> These descriptions are generalisations; they
> apply widely, yet don't apply to each member
> of their generational group.

It's also true that the more you know about the events that shaped each generation in their formative years, the better you'll be able to anticipate their responses.

Baby Boomers

Born 1946-1960

Baby Boomers were born between 1946 and 1960 and they are the largest population of any generation so far. They were born in the post World War II years when society was changing rapidly and yet when families and friends lived closely together and supported each other. The phrase 'baby boom' refers to a noticeable increase in the birthrate after the war.

On the whole, Baby Boomers were brought up with parents who gave them few choices, made decisions for them and expected them to 'do what you're told'. Thus the older Baby Boomers crave structure, rules, boundaries, consistency. In many families, the father was the breadwinner and the mother worked in the home, looking after the family.

It's surprising to many people today that when they were young Baby Boomers were idealistic, open-minded and rebellious – they rejected traditional values as teenagers in the 60s. Attitudes and behaviour shifted from what might be described as conservative to the 60s' Flower Power generation, the 70s' hippies and the sexual revolution. They were able to reap the benefits of abundant levels of food and clothes. Consumerism as we know it today began around this time.

But they became more conservative in their 30s and 40s. Job status, security and social standing are important to this generation – remember, they were brought up by Edwardians in families who had experienced two world wars. Perhaps it's a miracle then that Baby Boomers are so optimistic, ambitious and loyal.

In 2016 the oldest Baby Boomer will turn 70, while the youngest will be 56. The older Baby Boomers will have virtually disappeared from leadership roles in the workplace and it will be the Baby Boomer ll group, together with Generation X, who run the Boardroom.

In the UK, Baby Boomers were the first generation to be born in a free NHS hospital and to enjoy cradle-to-grave welfare; they were the first generation able to enjoy cheap foreign holidays – and many have retired on generous final salary pensions, the like of which we'll probably never see again.

Recently Baby Boomers have been divided into two subgroups as life experiences, attitudes, behaviours and society were very different in 1956 compared to 1946:

- Boomers I or the Baby Boomers, born 1946 to 1954

- Boomers II or Generation Jones, born 1955 to 1960 (from 'keeping up with the Joneses')

Baby Boomers – Characteristics

Core Values	optimism, generosity, achievement driven, involvement, loyal to careers and employers
Family Structure	mum, dad, children for most; divorce becoming prevalent
Education	highly valued; many achieved second level, few third level
Attitudes to work	quality matters, question authority, personal fulfilment, team players, entrepreneurial multi-taskers, strong work ethic
Communication styles	in person, becoming less formal, telephone, memo, fax
Attitudes to money	BB1: save for a rainy day; pay for things with cash. BB2: buy now, pay later
Work and family	Live to work. Little work-life balance
Motivated by	money, titles, recognition, being valued and needed NB dislike: feedback

The older Baby Boomers often stayed with one employer for all or significant amounts of their career. Their strong work ethic created the concepts of 'workaholic' as 'work came first'. Baby boomers are said to be driven to succeed, which can cause issues between them and their Gen X children, who have many different drivers and values.

Living longer means working longer.

By the time Baby Boomers ll came along in the mid-1950s, they became the first generation with TV; they were instilled with greater expectations and many aspired to achieve a level of prosperity they hadn't experienced at home. They became competitive achievers; this is probably why they're referred to as Generation Jones. Amazing things were happening in the world such as walking on the Moon, the sexual revolution, drug experimentation and events such as Live Aid in the mid-80s.

Famous Baby Boomers

Steve Jobs
Richard Branson
Arianna Huffington
Stephen Spielberg
Angela Merkel
Prince Charles
Oprah Winfrey
Simon Cowell
Meryl Streep

High levels of divorce have had an unexpected effect on the lives of many BBs. Their adult children are returning to live at home following marriage and relationship breakdowns. Many 'boomerang' Gen X children have experienced significant financial challenges given the recent recession, most notably the increase in house prices.

One of the interesting things about Baby Boomers has been their changing attitude to, and acceptance and use of, the internet. While many actively resisted it at first, this has changed with increased confidence in using tablets and the lower price of PCs and, pragmatically, because more and more services are moving online. Boomers are now comfortable with online and mobile technology (42% have a tablet) and they continue to be decision makers with significant influence, not to mention purchasing power.

> Mixed-aged teams ... are shown to
> increase the relative productivity of older
> and younger workers alike.

Generation X

Born 1961-1980

Typically both parents of Generation X children worked outside the home, so Gen X experienced three big differences compared to their baby-boomer parents: nursery school, relocation to the 'new towns' or cities and divorce. Gen X learned to be self-sufficient, independent minded and resourceful at a young age. They are the best educated of the three generations; many more Gen X went to university than the BB generation. In general Gen X are pretty sceptical of authority and more questioning of the status quo. Unlike the older Baby Boomers, they welcome change. It will be interesting to see if and how Gen X attitudes change over the next 20 years, as they become the 'older' generation.

In the UK they've been called the Maggie Thatcher generation; she encouraged entrepreneurship and people of Gen X responded; many have started and run several businesses (including this author).

Many experienced redundancy, the downsizing of organisations and the growth in technology which most likely provided the opportunity to harness their drive and 'go it alone'. Gen X are said to have created the 'work-life balance' concept. Like Baby Boomers, they show resilience and an ability to 'bounce back', survive and thrive, even in difficult circumstances.

Age discrimination comes in many guises. More often than not, it is the result of lazy stereotyping. So, the middle manager who feels threatened by a candidate with more experience than them, or significantly older or younger than them, or the recruiter who shows an unconscious bias towards candidates his or her own age, need to take care.

In 2011, the first Gen X turned 50 years old and the youngest turned 30. The majority of directors and senior managers in organisations are now Gen Xers, so they have significant power, control and responsibilities in the world of work.

In their private lives, divorce has hit this generation heavily and financially undermined many of them significantly. At the same time, one of the challenges they are currently facing is that of caring for aging parents while raising their children. Though they have a strong work ethic, many of Gen X are committed to their families or lifestyles and expect significant workplace flexibility.

Gen X differs from older Baby Boomers in the workplace in that they 'work to live' not 'live to work'. Gen X responds well to an unstructured, flexible workplace and they were the first generation to 'work from home'. They tend to change employment frequently, are not afraid to change careers and they will leave a job if they're unhappy or think a new way of working will give them a greater sense of achievement and make them happy.

Given that they are a driven generation, they are highly motivated to succeed; they focus on relationships, achievements and developing their competencies and skills. If you can harness their drive and abilities and retain them in your organisation, you have a valuable resource in them.

There is some truth to the benign view that many Gen Xers are willingly choosing to downshift, work less, and lead a more DIY lifestyle. In an era when steady employment is a struggle to find, more Xers are prioritizing time with their families over longer hours at the office. They see traditional full-time positions as a burden rather than a benefit. This is especially true for Xer men who are seeking to be much more involved fathers than their own parents were. (Reference: Forbes)

Generation X – Characteristics

Core Values	scepticism, informality, fun, take it as it comes, ask 'why?'
Family Structure	both parents working; therefore independent
Education	level second and most attended third level
Attitudes to work	not a job for life. A challenge, an opportunity to succeed. A contract. 'What's in it for me?' attitude, can be a stepping stone to somewhere else.
Communication styles	immediate, direct, email, texts, want structure and direction
Attitudes to money	cautious, save for what you want
Work and family	work to live, they strive for work-life balance, don't always achieve it. Divorce has had a significant negative effect on many Gen Xers
Motivated by	being entrepreneurial, doing it their way, freedom to act, success

Famous Gen Xers

President Barack Obama
Jeff Bezos – Founder of Amazon

JK Rowling
Kenneth Branagh
Friends
Quentin Tarantino
The Princess of Wales
George Clooney
Sheryl Sandberg – COO of Facebook and author of *Lean In: Women, Work, and the Will to Lead*

 Interesting statistic: Dale Carnegie Research has found that employees between the ages of 40 and 49 have the lowest levels of engagement.

Generation Y

Born 1981-2000

The selfie generation?

In 2016, the oldest in Gen Y are 35 years old, the youngest just 16 years of age. Since a significant number of them have yet to join the workforce and make their mark, commentators continue to watch and assess this generation and our understanding of them continues to develop and will do so for some years to come. Given this fact, I cautiously present the following for consideration and, given it's an evolving picture, recommend you keep an open mind and a healthy dose of optimism for what they can achieve and contribute to organisations. We don't know yet just what levels they can achieve.

The 'growing up' environment for Gen Y is markedly different from what went before. Many say Gen Y are overprotected and some would say over-provided-for – and they are certainly the most supervised generation so far. Seldom out of the sight of their (mostly) BB parents, Gen Y have been given choices all their lives; this is in stark contrast to older Gen Xers and BBs, who had decisions made for them. The paradox of choice is already looking as if it will become a significant issue for this generation in years to come.

Since they were born, Gen Y are said to have been given everything they want (and often things they don't want); they've been told 'you can do anything you set your mind to'. Over time, these messages sink in and become internalised and they are now perceived to have an overdeveloped sense of entitlement. Parents have raised their Gen Y children to value independence, personal aspirations and meaningful work.

It's not surprising then that Gen Y thrive on having a choice and options and consequently are confident at making decisions (I didn't say they're all good decisions). At the same time, the range of choices and possibilities is creating complexity and challenges for them that they may not yet be capable of managing. They crave positive feedback because they've been given so much encouragement and the message that 'you can achieve anything you put your mind to' by their parents.

At the same time, there is evidence to suggest this is another very entrepreneurial generation. Many shun working for large organisations and, instead, start their own companies at an early age. They have a greater acceptance of diversity and inclusivity, and are considered open minded and more accepting of differences in race, gender, ethnicity, and sexual orientation than previous generations. The question remains as to whether this will mean Gen Y are less competitive in work and life. Time will tell.

This generation came of age during the rapid growth of the internet and social media; the constant presence of technology means many have never known a time without a smartphone, social media and tablets. Many are more comfortable communicating via personal messaging on Instagram, WhatsApp, Facebook, Twitter, etc than they are face to face. It remains to be seen what impact this has at work as they climb the corporate ladder and become managers.

They are comfortable sharing their life, their thoughts and their reactions online. They are the first 'let's take a selfie' generation – perhaps they'll become known as the selfie generation?

One of the most fascinating – and possibly challenging – issues for the future of leadership in organisations is discussed by Sheryl Sandberg in her insightful and brilliant book *Lean In: Women, Work and the Will to Lead*. A survey of Gen Yers found that 'women were just as likely to describe themselves as ambitious as men… however, Gen Y women are less likely than their male counterparts to agree to the statement 'I aspire to a leadership role in whatever field I ultimately work'. They were also less likely than their peers to describe themselves as 'leaders', 'visionaries', 'self-confident' and 'willing to take risks'.

Warren Buffett, one of the world's most successful investors and one of the richest, said that 'the reason for his great success was that he was competing with only half of the population'. It was generous of him to say so, so it's not surprising, and yet wouldn't it be great if it were no longer true? Women are making slow if steady progress in moving up organisations and into leadership positions, but not as fast as was expected 20 years ago.

What a breakthrough it would be for global economics, as well as for women, men and organisations, if a way was found to engage and maximise the phenomenal potential of Gen Y, with all their motivations, values and aspirations. It falls to leader-managers who employ men and women to maximise each person's potential.

Generation Y – characteristics

Core Values	realism, confidence, what's next?, goal oriented, multitasking
Family Structure	wide mix of family makeup and blended families more prevalent
Education	an incredible expense (think student loans) – worth it for some, not for others
Attitudes to work	means to an end. Interesting while they are interested. Get bored quickly
Communication styles	virtual, immediate, smartphones, internet, social media
Attitudes to money	earn it to spend it
Work and family	balance, life-work predominance
Motivated by	workplace flexibility, visible career path, meaningful work, working creatively with others, opportunities

Emerging research is suggesting their willingness to work hard to achieve the lifestyle they want has been influenced by their baby-boomer parents. Gen Y consider work and life to be integrated; with technology, they can work from home, the park, or the office – and they're not restricted by the 9-5 culture, since the internet never closes. This attitude to work-life integration (as opposed to work-life balance) may be the case as they see work as less central to their lives than previous generations.

Research presented by *Forbes* suggests that 26% of Gen Y surveyed said that 'workers should only be expected to stay in a job a year or less before looking for a new position. 41% of BBs say workers should stay at least five years before looking for a new job; only 13% of Gen Y agree.'

In an article called 'Are millennials as bad as we think?' Tomas Chamorro-Premuzic suggests that Gen Y are complex and writes about the 'paradoxical nature of their character'. He suggests they are ambitious but lazy; hyper-connected but self-obsessed; hard to motivate but more engaged.

They are tenacious go-getters with an 'I can do anything' spirit, and they demand to be seen, be heard and be accommodated.

For these digital natives, online social networking sites such as Facebook, WhatsApp, Instagram and Twitter are vital forms of communication.

In short, it's looking like Gen Y has been pampered and programmed to overachieve since they were toddlers – they are both high performance and high maintenance. There's a general expectation of being rich and famous – look at the cult of celebrity – and there's some evidence that some of them are investing more and earlier than their BB parents.

The pertinent question for managers is: how can organisations leverage Gen Y's strengths, maximise their engagement and performance and retain them long enough to be worthwhile contributors, without paying the cost of their shortcomings?

Famous Gen Yers

Mark Zuckerberg*
Beyoncé*
Lady Gaga*
Andy Murray
Prince William
Catherine, Duchess of Cambridge
Taylor Swift

* *"These are among some of the top influencers among US Gen Y since they induced innovation across society and paved the way for a generation of individuals who seek to make a name for themselves too.' Huffington Post*

It is interesting to note also that although Steve Jobs and President Obama are not Gen Y, they rank highly on the list of people who reflect the spirit of their generation.

All in all then, the jury is still out on Gen Y. At the time of writing, there's a sense they're a Marmite generation. They are either admired or demonised and there's little written about them that falls into what I'd call a 'balanced perspective'. So we will have to wait and see. My bet is that they'll surpass our best expectations of them, in time.

And the story doesn't end there.

Generation Z

Born 2001–2020

The newest generation, Generation Z, were born after the year 2000. This generation are still being born, yet already there's speculation and some early indications about them.

This generation have never known a life without the internet, computers and smartphones. In the US they are also known as Digital Natives and are used to instant action and satisfaction due to internet technology. They are mainly the children of Generation X and are born into smaller families with older mothers. Communicating on Facebook, Twitter and Instagram, they are capable of belonging to huge communities and have massive collaborations using the internet without knowing anyone personally. Consequently, they prefer to conduct multiple conversations covering a multitude of topics over several minutes by messaging, rather than by face-to-face conversations. When they have questions, they 'Google' it. When they want to know how to do something, they find out how on YouTube.

But they're also growing up in a world shaped by 9/11, Columbine, IS and the War on Terror. They have a sense of social justice, philanthropy and maturity that comes with growing up during one of the most severe economic recessions in history. Early indications suggest they see themselves as the solution to these problems and, as a result, are more likely to pursue careers they think will help society.

There is some speculation that they may not perform well in areas such as public speaking, but this is yet to be proven. Much more will be written and understood about this generation in the next few years, as they join the workforce.

If you'd like to know more, check out http://www.slideshare.net/AENC/gen-z-final-white-paper

Speculative famous Gen Zers

Malala Yousafzai – Pakistani education campaigner who survived being shot by the Taliban and who became the world's youngest ever Nobel Prize recipient

Harry Styles – One Direction was the first UK pop group ever to debut at #1 in the US with a debut album

Selina Gomez – at 17 she became the youngest ever UNICEF ambassador

Prince George and Princess Charlotte of Cambridge

Arran Slaven – son of John, who is an avid learner, an effective leader-manager and great role model

Too young to remember 9/11, many of them played games on tablets before they could read. They are growing up in a world recovering from a major recession; a world full of turmoil, with cultural, political and religious divisions as never before. If Malala Yousafzai is anything to go by, they'll be a generation driven by making a difference, not accepting that things can't change. Sparks & Honey says 60% of them want to have an impact on the world, compared to 39% of Gen Y. This could be the impact of 'celebrity' as children of current celebrities carve their own way in the world, or it could be that many of this generation become famous for being famous (think Kardashians).

Tips on how to manage the three generations

When managing Baby Boomers ...

Remember, just like your generation, Baby Boomers differ among themselves. Identify whether they are more likely to follow your lead, rightly or wrongly, or whether they are more of a BB2 and will fight you every step of the way. Then adjust your approach.

Gen X managers of Baby Boomers

Explain the 'why' of how your ideas will work or why you want to change systems, processes, etc, and 'sell' the benefits and demonstrate rigour in 'how' the change will happen (to reduce resistance).

- Be careful of being seen to criticise Baby Boomers, who, you may consider, seem too conservative and reluctant to accept new ways of working

- They like to be appreciated (as with other generations) and being shown respect in small ways is important to them

- Ask their opinion; listen to what they have to say; engage them

- Resist the temptation to get frustrated with them if they express a differing opinion from you. They may have a point, whether or not you may wish to acknowledge it. Plan for it, discuss and debate it with them – and find some kind of resolution

Gen Y managers of Baby Boomers

- Ensure you gain their commitment and agreement to action. If they promise something, they tend to deliver

- Be careful of being seen to criticise Baby Boomers, who, you may consider, seem set in their ways. Instead engage with and encourage them to share their vast experience

- Show you respect, like and admire them

- Be willing to help them learn from you in areas such as technology

- Leverage their strengths, including work ethic, reliability, problem-solving approaches, accumulated knowledge and skill

- Be aware that Baby Boomers may have read that 'Most Gen Yers grew up in a warm, supportive environment in which they were constantly told they were the best or brightest, regardless of the facts'. Given Baby Boomers' work ethic, they will want you to prove yourself.

A manager I was coaching said to me recently that Baby Boomers annoy him. When I asked why, he said, 'Because they're so often right; sometimes I don't want to see it, don't want it to be that way; don't want to agree with them. They have an annoying ability to cut to the heart of the issue and suggest action that, even though they themselves don't like it, they know is the best thing to do.'

When managing Gen X

- Avoid micro-managing them – they appreciate their independence and because they are entrepreneurial and creative they are great assets to any organisation

- Be straightforward – they are confident, not afraid to debate, discuss and can take properly delivered constructive criticism

- Leverage their valuable experience and their capacity to excel as leaders within their current companies

- Appeal to their need to accomplish something beyond themselves

- Maximise their entrepreneurial spirit in finding ways to help the business innovate and grow while retaining your best talent

- Offer a variable work schedule – flexible hours or working from home where possible

- Recognise them for what they've achieved; they have proved their worth and are contributing significantly. Continue to engage, stretch and excite them

- Appreciate them genuinely and demonstrate respect in your dealings with them.

When managing Gen Y

- Remember that Gen Yers thrive in a fast-paced environment, and like structure and diversity of tasks to keep them interested and stimulated

- Get them involved in short projects with an end in sight; enable regular feedback to keep them on track and, where possible, offer flexibility in terms of working hours; remember they like options

- Baby-boomer managers need to be careful not to seem set in their ways; instead they need to encourage Gen Y input and spend more time coaching them

- They prefer to be managed and enjoy working in peer groups; they're much less self-motivated than Gen X

- Reward them for jobs and assignments well done. Acknowledge and give them recognition; they will quickly resent a boss who doesn't

- They want immediate feedback on how well they do a work task or project. They often respond poorly to constructive (and negative) feedback

- Explain why you're asking them to do something and tell them what's in it for them

- They value opportunity, not job security; they embrace corporate positions that promote social contribution and racial/sexual equality

- Helping them plan their career development will retain them longer; mentor and engage them

- They are more comfortable and confident communicating virtually so utilise their facility with social media

- While Gen X value change, Gen Y are addicted to it. Progressive companies will retain Gen Y by offering them ongoing training, consistent feedback on progress and immediate rewards for jobs well done

- Resist the temptation to 'put down' their ideas out of your ignorance of technology or discomfort with media technology. Use their knowledge rather than avoid it

- Tell them the truth; don't try to pull the wool over their eyes. They won't respect managers who aren't upfront and honest.

Future challenge for organisations:

Some analysts suggest that many in this generation will have 30+ jobs before they're 40 years of age. That will cost industry dearly if it comes true. (Reference 'Did You Know? 2014' on YouTube). If this proves true, what are the benefits and dis-benefits to your organisation, your recruitment procedures, your teams and your deliverables?

Competition between the generations

'Each generation goes further than the generation preceding it because it stands on the shoulders of that generation. You will have opportunities beyond anything we've ever known.' – Ronald Reagan

It's ironic given Ronald Reagan's insightful comment that it seems there are members of each generation who put colleagues in other generations down; find fault with them; deride and blame them.

This is a great shame and a real trap that managers can fall into if they're not careful. The trap is hearing and seeing the blame-game and failing to do anything to challenge it. Since you will have representatives of each generation working with you, you can examine your own conscience about this and consider where you stand and what you want your approach to be. Once you know this, you will be more able to challenge, debate, discuss – and it may need you to lead by example by demonstrating diplomacy and even-handedness (in the face of their defensiveness) and by finding the value in each person of each generation.

Age discrimination

One of the interesting things about making distinctions with age boundaries is that it opens up the possibility of each age group complaining about 'age discrimination'. Each generation blames another for this. Increasingly, Baby Boomers and older Gen X report feeling negatively judged and undervalued by many of their younger colleagues; while at the same time Gen Y report older colleagues making negative assumptions about their loyalty, experience, skills, etc.

Sadly, an article in *The Guardian* newspaper reports that 'despite a rising number of over-65s choosing to stay in work only a small minority of businesses are taking the issue of an aging workforce seriously'. Hopefully, as these numbers grow, more leader-managers will come to understand the implications of the "retention" argument made below and develop a greater commitment to breaking down the communication and to maximising the potential of their workforce, irrespective of age; otherwise they will find themselves short of talented workers their businesses cannot do without.

At the same time, and conversely, a recent 2013 Benefits for Tomorrow Study carried out by The Hartford found that almost nine in ten millennials (89%) agree that 'Baby Boomers in the workplace are a great source of mentorship' and that 93% of Baby Boomers agree that 'Gen Yers bring new skills and ideas to the workplace.'

Retention: The challenge for employers and managers

Retention of good performers and talented employees is a massive challenge in many parts of the UK at time of writing. For all the reasons captured above and the context of the recent worldwide recession, the costs associated with significant attrition is an issue most leader-managers will find themselves facing again and again in the years to come.

Will the attitude be 'attrition is a reality; let's accept it and therefore invest less in developing and retaining quality staff, since even if we do, they'll up and leave?' Or will it be 'we believe in attracting the best candidates, developing them and retaining them in our business'?

Retention – not just of people, but of knowledge, know-how, morale, productivity and talented workers.

> 'So why should employers care if employees in the different generations respect and understand each other? In a word: Retention. The costs associated with employee turnover are enormous (eg training, loss of employee morale, advertising for applicants, interviewing, productivity, etc). Gravett and Throckmorton estimate that costs to replace an employee may total up to 150% of the employee's annual salary, depending on skill level. In addition, the knowledge and talent that will be lost due to the retirement of the older generations without appropriate transition among generations could be financially devastating to companies. The employees coming into the labour force (Generation Y) are powerful in numbers and will be needed to make up for the shortage due to the retirement of the Baby Boomers and older Gen X. If employers don't help breakdown communication barriers now, they will find themselves short of talented workers when they are really needed.' Ref: http://bit.ly/1GkUIRO

TIP: Each generation has distinct values, attitudes, behaviours and expectations. Learn their drivers and use the knowledge wisely to lead and manage them successfully.

Maximising the potential of all

Latent potential is all around you in your organisation – across all three generations. Both men and women take on and stay in roles and perform well. There's too little focus on and belief in the real potential of every employee. The 'talent pipeline' in place in many organisations is often based on 'more of the same' rather than on looking wider and deeper into the skills and potential of others.

In search of more effective and efficient successful organisations, if you as a leader-manager can push some of the 'taken for granted' boundaries about people potential, we might move to a world where, as Sandberg says, 'A truly equal world would be one where women ran half our countries and companies and men ran half our homes.'

 What do you imagine would happen to performance and success across every organisation, if, as the laws of economics and many studies of diversity point to, all the resources we have were truly leveraged?

Ten tips for leader-managers (L-Ms) who are managing the three generations at work

1. Be aware that these are all generalisations about each generation, and even though these groups represent an approximate age range, members of these groups don't think or act uniformly.

2. The three generations have much in common – much more than they differ; remember there are some issues that affect all employees, regardless of age.

3. Understanding: learn about the different generations – what they share, what's important to them; how they differ; what they respond best to. You don't have to give them everything

they want but you'll be more prepared when you speak to them.

4. Manage the strengths and weaknesses of each generation. At the same time appreciate that each person is unique and has their own needs and drives. Be open to new ideas and explain the 'why' when discussing, debating and deciding.

5. Consider starting in-house company mentoring to help bridge the generation gap. For instance, a younger employee in a sales department can show a middle-aged peer how to use social media to draw in new customers, while a more experienced employee might help a less skilled person to practice face-to-face customer interaction.

6. Respect the value each brings to the team and business. Baby Boomers (BBs) have extensive knowledge and experience in changing contexts across 20 or 30 years; Gen X are entrepreneurial, innovative, highly motivated to succeed and willing to work hard; Gen Y are tech savvy, creative, energetic troubleshooters. If you can, harness their differences to drive progress and business results.

7. Avoid assuming that disagreement or conflict is about generational issues or age. It may be national or cultural. What I find interesting is that in their own ways, all three generations have a strong work ethic and are achievement driven in respect of what's important to them. BBs and Gen X both tend to respond to constructive feedback. Gen X and BBs have become adept at change – not because they necessarily enjoy it but because it's become a feature of the world they work in.

8. Be aware that the generational differences discussed here are generalisations and not absolutes. Lots of late BBs have become tech savvy; many Gen Xers are quite conservative and, like BBs, are highly productive and are motivated by money, titles and security of tenure. Significant numbers of

Gen Y are as careful with money as BBs were.

9. Create an open, inclusive and respectful environment where employees of all ages can bring their knowledge, experience and skills for the benefit of the business and without being judged, fixed or changed.

10. Avoid projecting your own generational expectations about work, workers, methods and personalities and stay open to the value that the different generations bring.

> Each generation has distinct values, attitudes, behaviours and expectations. Learn their drivers and use the knowledge wisely to lead and manage them successfully.

The current challenge is helping the three generations understand and communicate effectively and be productive while appreciating and acknowledging their differences.

Not only do Gen Y employees need to be understood and their potential maximised, but also, with more BBs and older Gen X working later in life, they all need help understanding and embracing the changes. Over the next 10 years Gen Z will become a presence in the workforce and it's possible that, for a time, three generations will become four generations at work.

The question you can usefully reflect on is how will you (and your company) engage, embrace, manage, promote and retain the complexities involved in order to leverage and maximise the benefits and reduce communication gaps.

If you are interested in exploring leadership from different perspectives, I recommend you take a look at a playlist of 12 TED Talks on 'How to be a great leader' here: http://www.ted.com/playlists/140/how_leaders_inspire.

In essence

You can decide for yourself to what extent you find these descriptors fit your experience. It's not an exact science but it does give you an overview of the societal changes that have taken place. And yet despite the differences, I see Gen Y employees identifying closely with Baby Boomer colleagues – both are entrepreneurial, they question authority, value personal fulfilment and have plenty to offer. Gen X and Gen Y value achievement and flexibility, so let's optimise the benefits that can be gained from this.

Another thing to remember is that people didn't change lock, stock and barrel between 1960 and 1961 and between 1980 and 1981. The changes happened over time and so it's wise to be cautious of defining anyone by the period they were born.

> Your challenge as a leader-manager is to understand the person in front of you while appreciating their values and the societal environment that shaped them.

- What is your experience of the three generations at work?

- Is there too little appreciation of what Baby Boomers know, have experienced, can continue to contribute to organisations (and society)?

- Can Gen X use their entrepreneurial, inspirational capabilities more effectively to retain people in the workplace?

- Are Gen Y so 'hyper-connected' that they display little interest in others except as an audience or is this too harsh a judgment?

- Is it true that because Gen Y seek 'work-life integration' they expect less from work and find fulfilment elsewhere in their lives? Is this OK, or can managers do something to shift their 'experience' in the workplace so that they find more fulfilment at work?

- Can and do the three generations work well together, despite their differences?

- If so, what implications are there for you as a leader-manager today?

Understanding all three generations for what they are and for what they can bring takes time and effort. If you want to attract, develop and retain them at work, remember you can't rely on the generalisations and prevalent stereotypes – you're best using the awareness as a benchmark on which to make your own assessment of an individual.

I recommend that you accept that people (whatever generation) are complex, valuable and full of potential and that if you invest the time to understand them, you will get a much more accurate assessment on which to base your approach to leading and managing them successfully. Your greatest contribution could be to create a place where people want to shine.

CHAPTER 2

Being a Leader-Manager (L-M) Today

Quick history lesson

Some years ago it was common for organisations to have 6 to 10+ levels of hierarchy. Managers managed people and process; leaders led the business, made the big decisions about strategic direction, hiring, firing and how to keep the business financially secure. Historically, those who led or owned the business were little in evidence on the shop floor. They had layers of senior, middle and junior managers and supervisors to make sure what needed to get done, was done.

In the last 20 years the landscape has changed significantly. Now it is more common for organisations to have 4 to 6 levels of hierarchy. Layers of managers and supervisors have been removed. The intention was to reduce expenditure on salaries and costs and 'do more with less'. This means that with fewer leaders and fewer managers, both leadership and management have been pushed down the organisation.

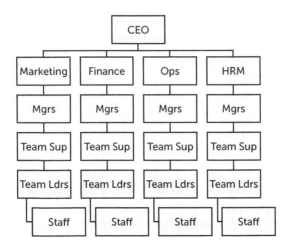

Fig. 1 Then (often 6 to 10+ levels)

The contracted organisational structures ended 'jobs for life' and the practice of promoting into 'dead men's shoes'. Nothing obvious was put in their place. Middle and senior managers were cut adrift – many retired early, others left and set up their own businesses – encouraging the entrepreneurial culture we now see around us. Downsizing became a new trend; those who remained were faced with managing a wider, more complex and larger group of employees.

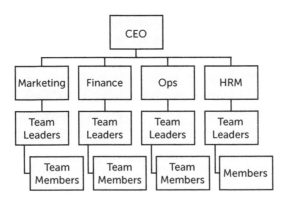

Fig. 2 Now (often 4 to 6 levels)

Those remaining were faced with fewer opportunities for promotion, more to do, less direct contact with their overseeing manager. They had to become more independent, self-motivated, engaged and accountable because the boss was 'busy with other things'.

Managers	Employees
Greater span of responsibility	Asked to do more with fewer resources
Fewer managers in org – more exposed	Multi tasking and broader job roles
Less day to day contact with teams	More autonomy / independence
Reduced loyalty to the organisation	Loss of sense of security / tenure
More to be accountable for	Less contact with immediate supervisor
Little support with the transition	Fewer promotion opportunities
Greater responsibility for same pay	More competition for promotion
Survivor's guilt	Tougher working environment
Competitive environment (peers)	Employment no longer felt secure
Threat of redundancy next time	Greater opportunity to visibly shine
Retention risk with better job offer	Increasing tendency to leave

Fig 3 Impact of downsizing on those who remained

The reluctant manager

Introducing the concept of leader-manager

Let's imagine you're qualified in engineering, accountancy, IT, the law, procurement, finance, bid management, HR, surveying, etc. Let's also imagine you've been working for a few years at least. You found yourself helping others to learn the job, then began overseeing their work, coordinating the work of a group of employees and, before long, were promoted and you became a 'manager'. This promotion is an opportunity to move up the organisation, comes with better pay and often attractive conditions. There's a sense of achievement and pride in being trusted to manage others and being given more authority to act, greater say in how things are done and access to a higher level of information than at operative level.

The challenge for many people who eventually move into management is balancing the fact that they originally became an engineer/an accountant/an IT specialist in the first place because they liked or loved that area of knowledge and work. When they become a manager of people, the time spent working on their profession reduces significantly.

Many professionals I've worked with over the past 20 years (such as accountants, engineers, HR, sales, IT, finance, psychologists, procurement, customer service, fund raising, design, marketing, etc) have been promoted to the level of manager and taken on responsibility for people. Some done this with conscious intent, some reluctantly and yet others in complete denial about the actual realities of 'managing others'.

The reluctant ones and those in denial want to believe they have a team of technical experts and 'talented employees who don't need managing because they're technical experts'. They say, 'My team don't need me to manage them, they know what needs to be done and they do it. I just report it upstairs.'

> When you take on the mantle of manager you,
> in effect, become a leader-manager.

However, these protestations don't mean he or she is not the team's leader-manager. If you manage others, then you lead others; you're a leader. The team look to you for leadership; they look to you to let them know, by word and deed, what is right, what is not; what's required; where the boundaries are.

Bear in mind that in reality, everything the leader-manager does and says, doesn't do, doesn't say, is noticed. There are few if any secrets. When you take on the mantle of manager you, in effect, become a leader-manager. The two are intertwined, inseparable and, throughout this book, you'll see how they are like two sides of the same coin.

Fig. 4 Leader-manager – two sides of the same coin

Do you feel drawn to one or the other? Are you an 'accidental' manager? Perhaps you think that to be a successful accountant/solicitor/engineer, etc, you can't be a successful manager? If so, you may experience a conflict with your own sense of identity. Are you an accountant or are you a manager? How can you be both? What would it take for you to embrace your inner manager and find a way to integrate it with your professional qualification? If you cannot, BE the accountant or BE the manager. Own your decision.

It is true that the vast majority of managers qualified in something other than 'management'. The advancement to manager is a common part of career progression. Consequently, when many professionally qualified and technical people become managers, they get the title, the job description, the team, the office/desk, the increase in pay. They may even be allocated a mentor or put on a management course to help them develop the necessary skills and self-awareness.

Yet irrespective of how well-intentioned the manager, being an effective leader-manager takes hard work, tenacity, practise and ongoing commitment.

It requires great planning, agility in handling different people and difficult conversations, the ability to manage resistance to change in a changing landscape filled with demanding employees and challenging clients.

> 'Credibility is the art of accepting responsibility.' - Julian Hall

Story: Alan is a geotechnical engineer who worked for an exploration and production company. Alan is a highly-qualified, highly-competent guy who loves the technical challenges that drilling the desert offers. He's highly analytical, single minded, process driven; there's nothing he loves more than being faced with what might for others be an insurmountable problem.

A couple of years ago Alan was given responsibility for managing the team he'd been working with. Previously the most senior person in the team, the team looked to him as their informal leader and he accepted this as getting the job done. However, at that time, he had none of the 'management' responsibilities – organising team meetings, communicating and dealing with the fall-out of organisational changes that impacted on team makeup and size. He abhorred having to conduct performance reviews (and often didn't bother doing them), setting annual objectives, managing underperformance, recruiting junior staff. Alan's defence against taking on a management role was that his technical skills and contributions would be reduced if his time was taken up with management/people issues.

Alan's director had a conundrum on his hands. Alan pushed back and he had a point. The director was forced to consider the pros and cons of having a very reluctant Alan managing the team while not contributing as fully to the technical issues facing the division in this constantly challenging arena.

It was a tough call. His director was sympathetic to the business case Alan submitted; at the same time he didn't want to encourage others to 'de-select' themselves from managing, which would undoubtedly generate its own problems.

Q. What would you do if faced with this conundrum?

As it happened, a colleague of Alan's was very motivated to take on a management role and, with extra support and development, this resolved the situation in a very elegant way. It might not have been so easily resolved.

Leader-managers can be faced with problems that make them feel 'I'm damned if I do, and damned if I don't'.

In cases like this the best solution is to consider all the factors and weigh their relative merits and costs – the whole picture needs to be considered. It's also important to act decisively and with conviction.

Defining the Leader-Manager roles

Here are a few (of many, many) activities managers of people are expected to do:

- plan, organise what needs to be done and when

- put people to work – allocate work, tasks, responsibilities; delegate to stretch and build capacity

- oversee the quality of outputs and processes

- monitor, review and assess progress

- manage performance – when it's good and when it's not

- set up reporting processes and ensure they happen
- have authority to make decisions within the scope set out by senior managers
- uphold the health, safety, quality, diversity, etc, standards of the organisation

Simply put, your work as a manager is to get what needs to be done done in the right way, at the right time and within budget, to the specifications agreed, through your team. So where's the 'leader' in this?

This of course will be for nothing unless the right person has been selected for the job in the first place.

In a London consultancy we worked with organisations to develop their managers to become more effective in four key areas:

- attract (select the right person into the right role)
- point (manage expectations and performance)
- develop (confidence and competence)
- retain (engage and motivate)

Balancing leadership and management

There's a prevailing assumption that managers only become leaders when promoted into very senior roles. I say we become leaders when we're promoted into management, as it is generally at this stage we have the authority to act on behalf of the organisation. If this idea gained more currency, those in senior roles could leverage this more powerfully and usefully, in service of the organisation's goals and targets. Managers are visible role models who represent the company both to internal staff and external stakeholders; they are, in effect, local leaders because they lead and manage.

Managers throughout the organisation contribute to leader responsibilities at a local level.

Activities and challenges requiring attention differ for leader-managers at different levels in the organisation. The direction of focus, time and effort will be influenced by both internal and external factors. Some of the elements that differ are:

Level of responsibility for decision making
Risk analysis and authority to take risk
Financial authority
Responsibility for getting work/delivering the work
Focus – strategic/operational
Legal compliance, health and safety, etc
Distance from where the work is carried out

The level of responsibility attached to the manager role changes as you progress up the organisation. The impact of decisions and actions takes on a whole new level at each echelon and the level of risk attached increases at the same time.

Additionally, the leader-manager balance during a calm and settled phase of business will be different from when the pressure is on to perform or when the company is under threat. Situational management. Situational leadership.

While working with large groups of very senior managers over the past five years we discussed several times their flexing of leader-manager focus (of time, effort, focus and responsibilities) and their views were as follows:

Job title	Leader	Manager
Team Lead	10	90
Team Manager	25	75
Departmental Manager	35	65
Divisional/Regional Manager	55	45
Director	70	30
Senior Director	75	25
CEO/COO	80	20

Fig. 5 In settled times

Job title	Leader	Manager
Team Lead	20	80
Team Manager	30	70
Departmental Manager	40	60
Divisional/Regional Manager	60	40
Director	70	30
Senior Director	65	35
CEO/COO/MD	85	15

Fig. 6 In pressured times

The groups' thinking was that when the organisation is threatened or under pressure, some roles put more focus on 'managing' and others shift into a higher gear of 'leading'. The highlighted numbers in Fig. 5 show these shifts.

Some of the flexing may seem counterintuitive. Senior levels needed to increase their management activities, while greater leadership was demanded at more junior levels since it was their responsibility to interpret how to make the changes happen while ensuring the 'headline message sent to all remains consistent across the business'.

 This is by no means scientific research – but I hope it gives you food for thought.

- What happens in your organisation?

- Where are you and how do you behave?

- Where is the balance of focus and energy between leadership and management – in settled times/in pressured times?

- Are these levels serving the company and its performance?

- What needs to change?

- Will the balance help sustain the company through hard times and help it be future-ready?

Maximising the 'potential' of having leader-managers

There is a difference between the role of leader and the role of manager. Their ultimate goals are the same: they are working towards organisational success and sustainability. However, their focus is different and complementary. Here are a few examples:

A Leader is responsible for:

- Setting direction and holding boundaries

- Strategic thinking, strategic planning, strategic decision making

- Having a clear vision and mission and communicating it

- Engagement of staff and clients

- Setting and maintaining the moral compass for the organisation

- Setting up and holding people accountable for their actions

- Knowing when and how to alter course

- Macro decision making

- Financials – setting, communicating, managing

- Setting and aligning business metrics… and much more (see assessment below)

A Manager is responsible for:

- Organising self and team to deliver

- Delivering the tasks, goals, targets

- Communicating so people get the message

- Dealing with, and resolving, problems and conflicts

- Monitoring progress and managing performance

- Maintaining discipline to deliver results

- Micro decision making within scope

- Overseeing quality

- Building the capacity of the team

- Upholding company policies and procedures

You can look at each of these in turn and see that, irrespective of your level of seniority in the organisation, you contribute to each example above, in one way or another – and that this contribution changes with context and seniority.

At a simple level, the leader's focus is more strategic; the manager's focus is more operational. The job of every manager in the organisation is to contribute to the holistic goals of the organisation that drive successful results and thus each manager has responsibility for their part in this contribution.

 Exercise - Assessing yourself as a L-M

Here you have a chance to consider the balance of your effectiveness. You can complete this exercise by yourself – and you also have an opportunity to copy the page and ask your key stakeholders eg peer, colleague in another dept, boss, client, direct report for their assessment.

Score: **1** = Consistently 2= Frequently 3 = Mostly 4= Sometimes 5 = Infrequently

Leader-		-Manager	
Demands robustness and rigour		Organises self and others to deliver	
Holds others accountable for doing what they commit to doing		Plans own and team's inputs/outputs	
Engages staff and clients		Communicates so people get the message	
Models company values; Demonstrate courage		Sets and communicates expectations and manages them	
Knows when to flex and when not to		Deals with and resolves conflicts	
Sees the big picture – having a clear vision		Uses influence and persuasion to deliver	
Plans and reviews - Is future orientated		Manages under performance proactively	
Sets direction; creates vision		Delivers tasks, procedures	

Understands connections between issues		Balances the delivery/profit cantilever	
Thinks broadly and strategically		Communicates direction	
Plans strategically		Explains the 'why?'	
Uses persuasion to engage		Sets SMART objectives and reviews regularly with others	
Knows when and how to alter course		Holds others accountable for their actions, achievements / lack of	
Understands implications of actions		Disciplines poor attitude, behaviour and results	
Sets and maintains the moral compass of the organisation		Upholds company policies, procedures	
Exercises fairness in practice		Monitors performance, attitude, behaviour	
Sets, communicates, reviews financials		Trains team members to deliver	
Understands concepts behind company policies and procedures		Builds the capacity of the team through coaching and delegating	
Makes macro decisions		Drives performance through motivation	
Demonstrates trust in others, honesty and integrity		Encourages willing followership	
Uses influence to inspire		Makes micro decisions	
TOTAL		**TOTAL**	

Fig. 7 Exercise - Assessing yourself as a L-M

When you've completed your scoring, add up the numbers. Remember to use the scoring above. When you have your total, you can reflect on where you consider you're already effective, where there's scope for improvement and action – and also what areas do not fall into the scope of your current level of responsibility. Finally, ask yourself 'How can I begin ?'

Beneath-the-surface drivers

There is an art to asking questions, and the ability to ask great questions is a core skill and a fundamentally essential one for manages and leaders. In many circumstances, people take a scatter-gun approach to asking questions – they emerge as a random collection of fragmented questions that jump from one thing to another. The usefulness of the outcomes can be just as random and unpredictable.

Socratic questioning (SQ), on the other hand, is a critical thinking approach that involves asking a series of questions on an issue in a systematic and disciplined way. The purpose is to get to the truth of things by uncovering assumptions and evidence, introducing alternative viewpoints by following a line of reasoning through the logical implications of the situation.

SQ methodology can be beneficial in many of the circumstances included in this book: managing performance; interacting with people who are resisting change; when managing the expectations of others – and more. If this methodology is something that interests you, you can research it thoroughly online.

My purpose throughout this book is to get you to ask and answer your own questions about your practice of leadership and management by making you think, connect and draw out the answer from yourself.

> The art of questioning is important to
> excellence of thought.

When I ask managers what's their number one key driver at work, many immediately say 'money', though others say a sense of achievement, sense of fulfilment, making a contribution, etc. When I accept that answer without comment and then ask 'What's important about achieving?' or 'What does having a sense of fulfilment make possible for you?' or 'What does having money give you ?' they begin to consider what's beneath the surface… what truly drives their work, their lives, their behaviour, their efforts. For instance, for many people, money is an enabler for other things that are important or vital, such as financial security, comfortable family life or stress-free quality of life. My grandmother used to say that 'money makes you more of who you already are'.

Knowing what drives and energises you gives insight into:

- how and why you do your job

- why you prioritise the activities you do

- what you avoid and the reasoning behind it

- what strengths you rely on (and which ones you over-rely on)

- what you choose (consciously or unconsciously) to spend your time on

- where you put your energies

Here are a few examples of motivational drivers:

- recognition

- appreciation

- responsibility and trust

- independence

- power and status

- authority

- camaraderie

- opportunity for self-development

- cooperation

- achievement

- contribution

Exercise - What invigorates you?

The purpose of this exercise is to help you understand what invigorates you; where you are with your own development; where the gaps exist and what you can do next if you choose to be a more effective leader-manager.

Scoring: Rank each statement as H = High   M = Medium   L = Low in terms of the extent to which it energises you and spurs you to action

	Score		Score
Establishing results and relationship driven interactions with team, clients – all		Solving the immediate problem – for client, team, boss	
Helping individual and team understand implications of their actions		Disciplining direct reports as and when necessary. Not shirking or delaying	
Acting with rigour and consistency in work and standards		Sharing information with the team	
Leading by example (especially when no one is looking)		Avoiding repetition of errors, mistakes, delays through effective training and supervision	
Avoiding jumping to too-early conclusions		Getting on with the delivery of the work	
Asking high quality questions that provoke new thinking		Acknowledging other's contributions	
Filling in the blanks (*see Disney story below)		Taking into account individual competencies, motivations, drivers as well as experience and despite job role title	
Listening first, then speaking		Consequences management; following up on and taking action on under performance	

Inspiring others		Not colluding with 'old guard' attitudes and behaviours	
Critically analysing data before deciding		Naming the issue and asking individual / team to work with you to resolve issue	
Balancing being firm, fair, focused		Being respectful of others as you'd like them to be of you	
Calibrating to others accurately		Managing your own state. Keeping confidential matters confidential for as long as necessary	
Encouraging healthy debate		Facing up to tackling issues you dislike, are uncomfortable or feel incapable of resolving	
Respecting others while disagreeing		Gaining satisfaction and pleasure from small and big successes – yours and the team's	
Being dependable		Being recognised for your contribution and that of your team – and knowing the difference	
TOTAL		**TOTAL**	

Leader			Manager		
High	Medium	Low	High	Medium	Low

Fig. 8 Exercise - What invigorates you?

Now reflect on how you scored yourself.

As you look over your responses, reflect on the extent to which you do these actions as opposed to how much you'd like them to be true. There's no benefit in self-deception. The truth may be uncomfortable at first, but it enables you to do something about it rather than stay trapped in the illusion.

High drive

These are the areas you indicate are important to you in carrying out your role. Reflect on how these serve you, the team, and the organisation. Also reflect on how easy or difficult it is to act on these – what makes it difficult? What are the conditions that allow you to act on them? Factors include other people; your confidence level; your previous experience in this context; how you're thinking about the context and assumptions you are making, etc.

Medium drive

These are areas that you have some drive/motivation towards. It may be because they are necessary and important to the role rather than areas you feel really driven to. These areas may also be relatively unfamiliar or unavailable to you in your current role.

Low drive

These don't inspire, galvanise or stimulate you. The question to ask yourself then is what difference does this make to my leadership, the team, the result, the organisation? Could it be a question of a lack of confidence, competence or familiarity? Explore and gain whatever insight you can – not to berate yourself, rather to ensure that these 'low drive' areas are covered by someone in the team or project.

Now look at the balance of High, Medium and Low drive areas.

- Are there common threads?

- What is your Low score? What is your Medium score? What are the implications for whether you're more 'leader' driven, more 'manager' driven or have a largely balanced drive?

- What actions or changes do you wish to make as a result of these insights?

  ○

  ○

  ○

* Disney : the story goes that when Walt Disney popped into creative planning meetings for future Disney movies, he looked/listened for three perspectives in the team: the dreamer, the critic, the realist. If he found an absence of any one, he would actively join the meeting, taking the part of the missing role.

In essence

- Everyone who manages people is a leader and a manager = leader-manager

- Flatter, lighter organisations require highly skilful leadership and management

- Many technical specialists promoted to L-M roles are in effect 'reluctant' people managers

- The L-M role today is a demanding one and is self-determined by the context and organisational culture

- The balance of focus between leadership and management needs to be fluid and determined by the situation

- Mental and behavioural agility will serve you well as a L-M in today's organisations

- Your L-M style is a function of how you live your values, your drivers and the culture of the business in which you work.

CHAPTER 3

Managing Expectations

When you, or others, are carrying out tasks that make up your job, there are four levels of achievement:

1. Missed the mark

2. A good try but not quite there

3. Got it done!

4. Exceeded expectations

As a leader-manager you will want everyone in your team and wider department to achieve level 3 or 4.

> 'People are not your best assets.
> Your best people are your best assets.'
> - Lloyd Vogelman

In order to set you and others up for success, clear communication is needed about what is expected, what the priorities are and what the protocols are when things go wrong. This is all about managing expectations and whose expectations am I referring to? Yours in relation to others who include your direct reports, colleagues, peers, clients, contractors, customers, etc.

Failing to manage expectations can be risky, while managing them effectively takes thought, takes focus and good communication (and can have its tricky moments); it is also incredibly valuable. It invariably leads to improved relationships, transparency, greater success and significantly less disappointment and frustration.

> The first step in exceeding your customer's expectations is to know those expectations.

The focus in this chapter is on managing the expectations of other people and the context is the workplace, although the principles below can be equally effective outside the workplace, in sport, home life, friendships and so on. We will explore:

- Why manage expectations

- When to manage expectations

- What is the psychological contract?

- How to communicate your expectations

- Preparing for clear, two-way expectations

- The expectations conversation

- What does it take as a L-M to manage expectations?

- Traps to avoid

- Conclusion/summary

WHY explicitly discuss and manage expectations?

In chapter 1 we explored the three generations at work and their differing values, expectations, characteristics and skills. We also acknowledged that within each generation, individuals are different, and in the context of performance, each person has their unique contribution to bring to your team. Everyone has individual needs and expectations.

How often do you stop and think 'How can I best manage A or B's expectations? How can I ensure that he's clear about my expectations? Probably not very often and not easily. And yet, actively considering whose expectations we need to manage, about what, and how best to go about it, is one of the most intelligent ways to manage your relationships. It will help you improve your interactions and should drive better performance.

As with so many management tools, the truth is that managing your own and managing others' expectations is easy sometimes – and it's tough at other times. I'm not saying it's easy; I am saying it's worthwhile, because something valuable always comes from clarity.

Consider: to what extent do you expect, hope or assume that members of your team will …

… know what I mean
… know better than to think that
… know what to do
… know not to do that
… know what not to do
… not need hand holding
… know what I expect from them
… know they can rely on me to…?

'We judge others by their behaviour.
We judge ourselves by our intentions.'
- Ian Percy

The reason I ask is that, generally speaking, we're not very good at mind reading – and in many situations we're equally bad at guessing correctly. One reason is because we have our own agenda running in our minds – and it isn't always the same as the manager's.

Another reason is that you assume that your team members will ask if they need help or don't understand something. If you examine your evidence of this, what is the reality in your experience? Some will. Some won't. If that equates to 50/50, then the assumption-reality gap could be significant in some contexts.

Fortunately, when you know the person or have worked with them over time, you'll probably become more skilled at guessing accurately. However, even then, you don't 'know' what's in their mind or what's on their mind, until they tell you or until you ask.

They may not consciously know themselves. Like you, they'll be on automatic pilot some of the time and the rest of the time they'll be doing their best to cope with working in a world that is changing constantly.

Managing expectations is part of the
psychological contract between you and
others you work with.

These are the reasons why one of the best practices you can apply as a L-M in your organisation is to get practiced and expert at discussing, agreeing and managing the expectations of others.

Sounds easy right?… And it is… with some people, in some contexts, especially with people you have a good relationship with; those you see regularly and can feed into the discussion. However, with other people and in other situations it is tricky and even difficult. But this doesn't mean it isn't worthwhile.

On the contrary, better to have the conversation and know where you both stand. Then later, you'll find it easier to 'update the conversation'. These conversations enable you to put a decent foundation in place on which to grow the working relationship. No foundation means no high-quality relationship. Managing expectations clearly is all in the service of making you and them more successful in achieving goals, targets and results. It's about setting up and keeping aligned to the psychological contract between you and others you work with.

> 'My job is to not be easy on people.
> My job is to make them better.'
> - Steve Jobs

It's surprising how often relationships with 'important others' for some reason don't fall into the 'easy' category (such as team members, boss, key client, key supplier, key contractor, senior influencers, peer colleagues, etc). Perhaps the working relationship is not what you'd like it to be; perhaps you don't see or speak to them with any regularity; perhaps you get on just fine, you leave them alone, they leave you alone; perhaps there's a clash of personalities; maybe you were promoted to a role they applied for; it's possible they take a different perspective from yours and fight you at every step of the way. Remember, all relationships are dynamic and 'stuff happens' that subtly or explicitly changes the relationship between you.

WHEN to have the managing expectations conversation

We live and work in a dynamic world and this means things are constantly changing around us. Sometimes we drive these changes, sometimes we don't. To reduce the chances of any nasty surprises, it's useful to assess the need to revisit the psychological contract between yourself and clients, direct reports, line manager, subcontractors, suppliers, colleagues, peers, client representatives, etc, and take the action when you determine it's necessary.

Here is a list of situations I brainstormed, where a conversation managing expectations would be useful. To be honest, even I was surprised by just how many there are on the list:

- in the early stages of a new working relationship and project

- when there are relevant or significant changes to how you work together

- when a new team member joins – and when existing members leave

- when there's a handover of responsibilities from one person to another

- when promotions take place

- when new processes/procedures are introduced and performance needs to change

- at regular intervals during a long-term project or joint venture partnership

- when there's a downturn in commercial success

- when something more or different is needed from employees

- when authority levels or reporting lines change, eg you're promoted over peers or vice versa

- when people fail to be accountable for what they've been asked/agreed to do

- when the level of performance is below what is expected/ what peers are achieving

- when attitudes in the workplace are getting in the way of delivering results

- when there's a failure to act after you've given them early warning about behaviour/attitude

- when levels of authority change/responsibilities are re-allocated differently across the team

- with a client who's in power mode (i.e. they're pushing through boundaries agreed earlier)

- where there's a lack of trust or where trust has been damaged

- where you cannot deliver or perform as agreed (reasons could be financial, geographical, contextual, situational influencers, etc)

- in the midst of organisational or departmental change that you're not driving

If you think you haven't the time to manage expectations in these situations, think about the cost of dealing with the consequences of not communicating and agreeing any changes that need to take place.

> Think about the consequences of not communicating and agreeing changes to expectations.

WHAT is the psychological contract?

Every time you move to a new job or to a new company, one of the first things you do is sign a contract of employment. This lets you know what the 'terms and conditions' are; what's expected of you; what you can expect of the company and when. It will tell you your job title, how much you'll be paid, where you'll work.

Most of us put these contracts away and never look at them unless something goes badly wrong or you're planning to leave and want to find out how much notice is required. It contains all the legal stuff you and the company need to cover most employment situations.

In order to avoid guessing, misunderstanding, mind-reading and the plain hand of fate, here's how you can avoid the pitfalls and show yourself to be a true L-M who has the courage to have a clear and open conversation and get expectations out on the table for everyone to see and agree. When you do this you'll have a much more robust psychological contract on which to build your team and the key relationships that drive successful performance.

The psychological contract is a trust agreement between two people and it is different from the contract of employment, which is between a person and an organisation. The psychological contract exists whether or not it has been discussed or thought about. You expect things from your manager, from your organisation, and in return they expect things from you. More often than not, these 'things' are implied and you're expected to deduce the subtleties from what has not been said or discussed. Additionally, therein lie lots of assumptions – a sure-fire recipe for misunderstandings and miscommunication.

To develop the psychological contract a conversation for shared clarity is required. A couple of hours invested at the start (or re-start) are worth their weight in gold in terms of buy-in, engagement, conflict avoidance, driving success and performance.

> The psychological contract exists whether or not it has been discussed. If it hasn't been discussed, the likelihood of having trust-gaps is massively increased.

In an ideal world, this early conversation will be a clear, specific, well-prepared-for, shared discussion with clear outputs, priorities, contingencies and an agreed way forward. You will leave the conversation knowing specifically what your line manager or subordinate expects of you and what they don't – and you will have shared your part too. These 'working together' boundaries will be the foundation on which your working relationship can grow.

This conversation is an important part of the early discussions between the line manager and the individual – and it would then be extended to include the immediate team and eventually all key stakeholders. The psychological contract is all about behaviours, what you are expected to do/to achieve/to not do/to prioritise; what to do when you don't know; how you work together (when things are going well and when they're not); how issues get resolved.

The psychological contract is a trust agreement.

The significant difference between the employment and psychological contracts is that the latter is not a legal document; it's a trust agreement and it will change over time, as the work situation, priorities and objectives change.

The purpose of the psychological contract is to set the underlying relationship up for success, to build trust and instil confidence and dependability in how each person relates with another.

So you have your employment contract and you start your job. You'll then spend the first six months or so getting to know what the job entails, making a good impression, establishing who the people are and how they work. It's exciting.

During that time you'll meet people you get on with and work brilliantly with, and others who are a pain in the proverbial.

At work, you'll meet people who are:

cooperative	productive	ignorant
willing	shy and withdrawn	unpredictable
helpful/friendly	quiet	manipulative
mild mannered	unhelpful	aggressive
dependable	contrary	hostile
industrious	uncooperative	dissatisfied/
supportive	demanding	demotivated
self-motivated	insistent	belligerent
resourceful	competitive	and more

Over time you'll know who matters to you, in terms of having an effective working relationship with them, and who doesn't.

 Activity – take an A4 sheet of paper

Stop for a moment now; take a sheet of paper and answer these questions – write a list of answers for each question:

Q: Who do you want to have an effective working relationship with?
A:

Q: Who do you want to have a MORE effective working relationship with?
A:

Q: Who do you need to have an effective working relationship with?
A:

Q: Who do you need to have a MORE effective working relationship with?
A:

Run your eyes down the lists again and put a 'tick' against each of those people you are working with now, separating them from others you will soon be working with. As a L-M your job is first to deal with those you're working with now; to get the best from them and to work effectively with them.

Fig. 9 Activity: Effective working relationships

You will always work with people who are helpful and dependable and others who are aggressive and uncooperative. As a leader-manager, if you can be agile at relating with and working with all, you will be more effective at dealing with the difficult people.

Keep a range of these people in mind as you read this chapter, so that you can compare and contrast as you reflect.

When you describe someone as 'difficult', what do you mean? They're the ones who fight back, are disagreeable, belligerent, have their own agenda, wont 'play the game', won't listen, say one thing and do another, etc … consistently.

This means there's a gap between you. It may be to do with tasks, responsibilities, solutions or more deeply-held values. This gap is the 'differing expectations' gap. That's what we're exploring in this chapter.

> The purpose of the psychological contract is to
> … build trust, increase empathy, instil confidence
> and actively encourage dependability.

If you have a how-we-work-together contract with your key stakeholders that defines the rules and boundaries of how you work, things will be clearer and will enable real synergies of production without the time wasted in competing, hidden agendas and arguing, all of which have negative emotions and costly results.

The psychological contract sets out how you'll work together effectively to achieve results; it will include agreements about what happens when, so that both parties have a shared understanding of how best to make it work and how to handle it when things go wrong.

> To develop your trust contract, a conversation
> for shared clarity is required.

Who should you have this level of conversation with?
Your line manager, your direct reports, long-term/repeat clients, key suppliers, peers, coach, mentor and colleagues you work closely with, subcontractors – and anyone else you consider to be a key stakeholder.

HOW: Discussing and managing expectations

1.1 Your preparation activity
Analysing/assessing levels of shared clarity

A key ingredient of effective working relationships is clarity of role and personal accountability. Given the complexity and dynamic nature of our working environment, boundaries, responsibilities and personal accountability are not always as clear as they should be. This leads to conflict, misunderstandings, arguments, mistrust, hidden agendas, splitting within teams, divided loyalties and uncooperativeness.

The process below is designed to bring people working together (including teams) through what Tuckman calls the 'storming' phase. (From: Bruce Tuckman's Team Formation Model. The stages are forming, storming, norming, performing, adjourning).

 Activity – take an A4 sheet of paper

1. Your first action is to stop and think. Using Pareto's 80/20 rule, write a list of the 20% of people you work with in order to achieve 80% of your results.

Include your line manager, up to four direct reports, a selection of active peers, clients, customers, suppliers and contractors and colleagues.

If your list exceeds eight people, use the 20% rule again, i.e. include those that are most important to work with in order to achieve 80% of the work.

Fig. 10 Activity: Write a list of stakeholders

Moving towards clarity using managing expectations conversation process

The first step in exceeding your customer's expectations is to know those expectations.

Using those on your 20% list, consider what you need from each person and what they can expect from you, in the context of the working relationship you have (or wish to have) with them.

It's helpful if you make it visual. If you like this idea draw three columns:

Column 1: Stakeholder Name
Column 2: What do I need or expect from you?
Column 3: What can you expect from me?

Complete the questions for one person at a time.

Preparing to Discuss Expectations		
Key Stakeholder Name	What do I need from or expect of them ? and Why?	What can they expect of me ?
	• • • etc	

Fig 11 Preparing to discuss expectations

Preparing to Discuss Expectations		
Key Stakeholder Name	What do I need from or expect of them ? and Why?	What can they expect of me ?
My Boss (Name)	clear objectives for key tasks, help with prioritising, if I'm doing something wrong tell me not others; regular (at least monthly) feedback on my performance, regular discussions and progress reviews, help dealing with difficult client; willingness to listen when I have a problem or want to discuss an idea; fair treatment; open and honest conversations about work, progress, issues, challenges, opportunity to play to my strengths; training when I need new skills; opportunity to progress and develop when I've proved I can achieve more.	work hard, do my job, turn up and be present, work cooperatively with others, ask for help when I need it, I'll ask for feedback on what works and what doesn't in our relationship, ideas, suggestions for improvements, tell you before others if there's a problem between us, support you in achieving your goals, be willing to go the extra mile when times are tough, develop my skills and knowledge, push for promotion when I think I'm ready, be honest in our conversations even if that means it gets sticky or difficult

Fig. 12 Preparing to discuss expectations – an example: for a conversation with your boss

1.2 Their preparation activity

When you're ready to set up a conversation, here's how to help it go well.

In advance of your conversation with a colleague, direct report, line manager, supplier or internal customer, follow this process:

1. Be clear about **what your intent is** in having the conversation, so that you can express it clearly.

2. Two to four days in advance of your meeting, see (or, if you can't, speak to) the person and outline your reason for requesting the conversation and share what you can both get from it.

If they agree, continue to 3. If they don't, either the time isn't right, or the relationship isn't ready. This needs to be addressed before you can continue.

3. Explain that you'd like to use two simple questions as a basis for the discussion. Share the two questions you have typed for them on a sheet of paper, one at the top, one halfway down. Give them the sheet or send it to them.

    - What do I need or expect from them?
    - What can they expect from me?

    Ask them to reflect on their answers and to write them down prior to the conversation.

4. Explain that you both carry out the same preparation so that you can discuss what comes out when you get together.

5. Agree date, time and place to meet. Reassure them that this is an 'exploration' and shared discussion and not something to be feared.

6. Do your preparation. Find the facts. Support with evidence. Consider alternatives. Empathise with the person you'll be meeting with.

Uncommunicated expectations are
resentments in the making.

1.3 How to handle it on the day

Start the conversation by building rapport, thanking them for their cooperation. Start by reminding both of you why you're here and what your shared purpose is. In this way, right from the start, it's a combined effort with mutual benefits.

Remember that your behaviour will influence theirs, so be empathetic ('It's a bit strange for me too'), warm, relaxed and open as you encourage a helpful exchange of views.

Something that can really help is sitting beside each other or at right angles while you have this discussion. This is less confrontational than sitting opposite and it's easier to share your notes, which builds trust and demonstrates openness. As soon as you're both ready, start the process.

If either of you is cautious, defensive or distrustful, reinforce the mutual benefits, 'The whole idea is that we discuss this openly and find a way that we can work together that works well for you and for me. If either of us holds back, it just won't be as good an outcome for either of us.'

As soon as you're both ready, start the process and if possible continue through steps 1 to 3 below. *'Shall we make a start and see how we go? Let's start with you. What were your thoughts?'*

If the other person is still very wary or hesitant, you may choose to ask the question: *Shall I go first or will you?'* instead of getting them to start. [In which case you'll do 2 then 1 below.] By starting, you show them how it's done; you model respect, cooperation and show that it's not a process of criticism or complaint; rather one of finding a way to express both sets of needs and expectations with a view to coming to clarifying and agreeing 'how we'll work together well and achieve success'.

If this conversation is with a direct report, I recommend you ask them to start. Otherwise there's a good chance that whatever they end up saying will reflect what you said and you may not get a true sense of their real thinking. Be very encouraging and non-judgmental as they start; it will feel risky, so your job as a leader-manager is to put them at their ease so you both get the most out of this conversation.

1. They share...

- What they need/expect from you (in whatever the working relationship is)

- What you can expect of them

Listen to understand. Avoid interrupting as they describe and share their thoughts. Ask questions for clarification. Ideally, it's best to keep discussion, challenges or feedback to a minimum at this stage. You will do this later.

2. You share…

- What you expect/need from them

- What they can expect of you

At this stage, ask them to listen, to understand and agree they will only ask questions for clarification. Agree that they'll keep discussion and feedback to a minimum at this stage since this will happen later.

3. Then…

When both parties have shared their thoughts you have an opportunity to discuss one another's input. Start by finding what you have in common. Reinforce these shared foundations. Then discuss any areas of difference that have arisen – are these real areas of difference or is it more to do with how they are described? When you clarify these questions, you can then move on to agreeing how the differences in expectations will be resolved or handled. Discuss when a follow-up would work. Diarise a date and time there and then.

4. Follow-up…

It works well to follow up this initial conversation, when both have had a chance to reflect on what was discussed. It may be that some areas could not be finalised in the first discussion, but can be signed off at a subsequent conversation.

Remember this managing expectations conversation is all about building a working relationship that will serve you both well over months or years. This process can be likened to building a savings account; your discussion is an investment in the relationship – and it is a great way to add credit to your 'joint account'.

Discussing and managing expectations is an
ongoing process NOT a one-off conversation
at the beginning of a contract or project.

Something else to be aware of is that team members, targets, processes, budgets, performance measures, timings, quality levels and performance requirements all change over time and so just like our tablets and computers, we need to 'install an update'. What I mean by this is that it works well to check back in with each other to update expectations by renewing the psychological contract. Review what stays the same, what changes, when, who, how, etc.

By the way, this process works particularly well when the answers are put on flipcharts, where you can both stand back to see what's been said. However, if this is not practical, then sharing the notes on an A4 sheet can also work very well.

What is essential is that both parties write down the answers to the two statements before you meet and share the contents at the meeting.

Sound advice: Your thoughts are just thoughts.
What you 'think' about yourself or others isn't
necessarily right or accurate.

Traps to avoid when discussing and managing expectations

Avoid assuming...

- that 'it's obvious, isn't it? I shouldn't have to spell it out' (it isn't and you do)

- that because you said it, they heard it, they get it, they agree

- because you said it once, they'll remember it (ref: the forgetting curve, Ch10)

- because you know them, you don't need to be explicit about it (you do)

- 'I'll do it when we do the annual review'. Do it now, review it then

- they can pick it up from their colleagues – it's too big a risk

- it's not much different to how we worked on the last project/ last year

- because they know us, they don't need to be explicit

- others will mind read accurately what you need and expect of them

In essence

- Your best people are your best assets. Your best clients are also your best assets

- Failure to manage expectations can be risky. Conversely, investing in your relationships can prove to be a great benefit if you do it before it becomes critically important

- Everyone has individual needs and expectations. If you don't know them, you're unlikely to meet or exceed them

- Most human beings are poor-to-awful at mind reading – all the more reason to investigate and share. At a very minimum, it saves all the guesswork!

- Virtually every time you have a conversation about expectations, you'll find out something you didn't know. Information is power

- The psychological contract is a 'trust account' between two or more people

- The consequences of not communicating and agreeing new and changed expectations can be serious for your business and your reputation as a leader-manager

- Empathy is one of the foundation stones of effective relationships. This works to your advantage too

- Remember, discussing expectations is an ongoing process, not a one-off. Repeat often – and integrate into your PDP/PDR/annual appraisal discussions.

CHAPTER 4

Think and Plan Before You Act

The only place where success comes before
work is in the dictionary.
– Vidal Sassoon

Life in the workplace is busy and sometimes relentless. Our time is filled with meetings, reporting, preparing, travelling, delivering results and managing tasks and people to such an extent it seems there's little chance to stop and think. At the same time, you are probably expected to do your preparation, but there's little visible encouragement or space to take time out of 'doing' to think and prepare. This, combined with a meeting culture, is fatal for productivity. It's easy for employees to become busy fools.

I frequently hear managers, when scheduling meetings with me, say, 'I have a meeting from 10am for an hour. I'll meet you at 11am.' If they stopped and thought about it for a moment they'd know this is bonkers. Apart from the fact that the first meeting might run on, this back-to-back scheduling means they haven't a moment to breathe.

Some people may be impressed by their 'busy-ness'. It would be better if they kept 30 minutes between meetings, to review the meeting, diarise actions, take a mental and physical breather, then 'get present' and refocused, ready for the next meeting.

How often do you hear people (including yourself) say things like …?

> *'If only I'd had time to sit and think about this before I said no'*
>
> *'He didn't give me a chance to consider the full implications'*
>
> *'I only had 24 hours' notice of going to that meeting; I had no time to read up on the issues'*

It would have been different had you/they …

… replied, 'I need a couple of hours (days) to think about this before I get back to you'

… said, 'I need time to consider the full implications – how genuinely urgent is this decision?'

… protected one hour to read the file; discovered the key issues in the light of current information and discussed what approach to take

Being busy is not the same thing as being productive. Some people lurch from one call or meeting to another, with little prep, with little input and often little output. They're so busy going to meetings they haven't time to action tasks that need to be done and that leads to other issues (discussed elsewhere in the book).

Q. So, what is the antidote to 'busy-ness' that surrounds you as a leader-manage that can help you lead by example with greater efficiency and effectiveness? Here are a few things to consider and apply in your role as leader-manager.

Be prepared for the unexpected

Why do you need little strategies, phrases, questions to pull out of your hat when the unexpected occurs, or when you feel you're being put under pressure to do something or make a hasty decision?

Because the unexpected is just that – it comes out of the blue; and often because it comes from more senior people we feel we can't refuse; because we are kind and others take advantage. But you deserve to take time to think and plan before you act or decide.

When these things come out of the blue we can feel pressured, embarrassed, wrong-footed, even compromised. This starts the heart beating faster; stress hormones explode around the body; and under this kind of pressure it can be hard to think clearly. That's a major reason why you need time to think; a breathing space. Time to quieten your mind. Time to get clear on the issue at stake. Time to plan your approach. Time to gather your evidence that may be mental or physical or both.

Remember, every decision, every action you take at work is, as a leader-manager, on behalf of the business. And most actions you take are noticed by others around you. There are few secrets in a team.

Outlook calendar entry:
Meeting 60 TPT = 60 minutes of 'think and plan time'

When you take time for think and plan time (in my diary *Meeting: TPT 60* means 60 minutes of 'think and plan time') before a meeting, an interview, a team talk, a meeting with a client or your boss, you put yourself back in control. You walk into the meeting or talk in a different manner; you give off a different vibe – and because you now know exactly what you want to say to start off, you look and sound much more in charge. This builds your confidence and your credibility in others' eyes.

Taking time to plan and prepare beforehand is a matter of self-discipline … and sometimes it needs confidence too.

Story: Sarah was with a major client waiting for her boss, John, to arrive; traffic had been hell on the M25. Then the call came that he was stuck behind a major accident; the motorway would be closed for at least two hours; he wouldn't make the meeting that was due to start ten minutes ago. Sarah was quick on her feet and said, 'John sends his apologies' (they knew about the motorway). 'I'd like to take ten minutes to speak to John to get clear on my lines of authority and to review our preparation notes and then we can begin. Is that agreeable with you?' They all agreed. Sarah took the time to speak to John – and some time to get her head straight and to take a few deep breaths. The meeting went well, partly because she composed herself well and wasn't afraid to say, 'This is something that will need to be parked until our next meeting or be signed off by John after further discussion.' Everyone at the meeting knew Sarah didn't have the same level of authority of decision making; at the same time, she nevertheless demonstrated competence, confidence, credibility and presence of mind.

Why think and plan well before acting? In order to set yourself and others up for success; to build and maintain your credibility; to represent yourself, your department and your organisation to the best level possible. Every time.

'One thing I learned from John is to do
my prep. He never went into a meeting
unprepared and it saved our bacon many a
time in sticky client discussions.'
– Mike Evans, Team Leader

Seven strategies to help you be more effective

Be deliberate

This intention encourages/forces us to pay attention to the detail and the reality, rather than doing what you always do or just leaving it to chance or instinct. It increases credibility.

When we show we've prepared well, we lead by example, encourage others to do the same. Good preparation influences the quality of the discussion and the quality of the decisions made. Leading by example also mitigates the 'if they can't be bothered to plan for the meeting, why should I?' attitude.

> I deliberately want to run this by you before I take it to the client/project manager/team to get your views.

Being deliberate and focused engenders engagement and re-engagement of demotivated or 'at risk of retention' members of the team, which benefits the team and the business.

Planning your approach with others who are involved (whether they will be present or not) encourages participation and breaks down barriers and silos, and leads to synergies that would otherwise not be evident or present. Combined action and layer upon layer of input leads to more ownership, better information … and cost effectiveness.

Story: Donald is a project manager – he's outgoing, ambitious, articulate and a driven Gen Xer. Five successful years in the US have built his confidence. Recently, he returned home to work in Ireland in a senior role. Everything was going well, with one exception. He found dealing with his introverted manager quite frustrating. It seemed their contrasting styles put them in conflict much of the time. When Donald proposed new methods and ideas, his boss frequently went quiet and replied either, 'I'll think about it' or 'Leave it with me'. After months of avoided conversations and a greater absence of proactive support and proactivity, Donald was considering leaving the business even though this was not what he really wanted. Fortunately, he discussed this with me in our coaching and together we explored his boss's style and communication preferences. Donald realised that his boss is highly introverted and reflective. At once, he deliberately went into research and thinking mode to investigate approaches and strategies he could take to improve the relationship. Over a couple of months he demonstrated agility in his thinking and behaviour in how he approached and worked with his boss. Things didn't change overnight, but Donald found these worked to a sufficient level; he and his boss have now developed a satisfactory way to work together and Donald is making an impressive contribution to the business.

Encourage consistent behaviours

'We are what we repeatedly do.
Excellence, then, is not an act, but a habit.'
- Aristotle

Reliability and consistency often go hand in hand and, according to social psychologists, commitment is the key element that reinforces the behaviour of consistency. Consistency is allied to dependability which is in turn allied to trust; these values are highly regarded by society.

Think about the time when you took a stand over a particular issue – with a boss, client, colleague. Isn't it true that once you had taken the stand, you had a strong tendency to behave in ways that were stubbornly consistent with the stand? You had committed to something and you wanted to demonstrate your consistency (to yourself and/or to others).

The truth is we like to be trusted in what we say and in what we do – and we like other people we are dealing with to be consistent too. Teams work more effectively and productively together when trust and consistency are present.

> 'Once we have made a choice or taken
> a stand, we will encounter personal and
> interpersonal pressures to behave consistently
> with that commitment.'
> (Cialdini, 2009, p 52)

Doing what you say you will do, when you said you would. Being a L-M is about leading by example, especially when no one else is looking. The challenge around consistency is that we live and work in a dynamic and changing environment and so a L-M needs to be able to juggle adaptability and flexibility alongside consistency. No one said being a L-M was easy. As with every role in life, it comes with its delights and its challenges. If you want consistency from others, being clear about what you believe consistency looks like in that context is more likely to get it.

> *Getting people to answer 'yes' makes them more powerfully committed to an action, Cialdini says. For instance, instead of saying, 'Please call if you have to cancel', asking 'Will you please call if you have to cancel?' gets customers to say yes, and measurably increases their response rates. Apply this principle in your team by asking your team members if they'll support your next initiative and say why.*

If you want others to do what they say they will, when they said it, what's the best way of encouraging it? By gaining their public commitment to action. Before you ask for that, discussing it with them and finding out what the obstacles are to doing it and doing it on time will also help. Once the obstacles are out on the table, you can facilitate a discussion with them about how they'll deal with them. People need time to think. Not just to react. Helping others develop their thinking skills is one of the greatest gifts you can give.

People need time to think; not just to react.

Maintain standards

Fig 13   5W1H

Every business has standards by which they measure success: income, profit, employee retention, quality, productivity, health and safety, public recognition, client retention, business growth, to mention just a few.

Every business needs leader-managers to set and maintain these standards, otherwise an environment of uncertainty and chaos is created and this inevitably shows up in performance and results.

Ask 5W1H

This is a simple methodology to help you set and maintain standards as you communicate to your staff. Each time you establish new standards – or when you need to hold people to account when they fail to deliver – use 5W1H:

Who, What, When, Where, Why and How

Story: Steve is the dealer principal at a large Japanese retail motor franchise – this means he runs the large dealership. Kaizen (continuous improvement) is a core value of the company and each dealership commits to apply Kaizen in everyday life. One way Steve chose to engage the team in Kaizen was by organising monthly Kaizen group meetings. One representative from each department plus managers attended. One day, the after sales representative (ASR) failed to attend the Kaizen meeting. As it happened, Steve joined the meeting for ten minutes as a show of support. He spotted the missing group member. After the meeting he went straight to the after sales manager (ASM) and asked why his ASR had failed to attend. The manager replied that he was with a client.

Steve could have accepted this. After all, clients are king. But Steve didn't accept it. He explained to the ASM that if he accepted that excuse for him and others, Kaizen would never be implemented. Steve reminded the ASM that it was his job to run after sales in such a way that company values are upheld – and in this context, this meant ensuring his team attended Kaizen group meetings. Steve used the 5W1H with the ASM. The ASR never failed to attend future meetings.

Be assertive

Imagine you had promised your operational team you'd respond to their third urgent request for more IT resources today. The decision hasn't yet been made because you've been re-working a bid for a major new contract that's due for submission in two days.

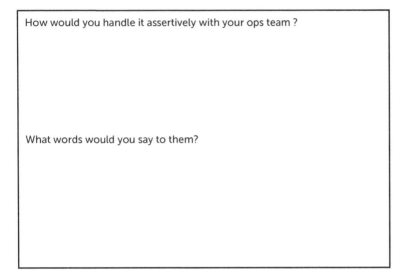

Fig 14 Planning to speak assertively

For some leader-managers this is a good example of 'values in conflict'. One value is about consistency in doing what you said you would and communicating with the team. The other value is about contributing towards financial success of the business. The challenge for the leader-manager is to balance the immediate and longer-term needs of the business with the practical IT needs and the potential 'demotivational' effect of not doing what you promised.

It's not the decision that matters most in this example – it's not about how perfect a L-M you aim to be. Some things are outside your control and a significant challenge that L-Ms face is weighing up competing priorities and making the best possible decisions in the circumstances. In this case, loss of a major client project would put employment at risk and then the need for extra IT resources would be a moot point.

How you handle it with the team is the difference that makes the difference in this kind of situation.

Before you act think and plan:

1. what you want to say and

2. how you will say it before you get the team together

Being honest and open, handling it well by presenting the situation and the commercial risks, acknowledging the dilemma and explaining your decision without embarrassment will ensure you demonstrate respect for them linked to commercial pragmatism. People know that these things happen. They understand; especially when it's presented properly. It's when it's not that you get push back, resentment and whinging. You have a choice. You can be clear and assertive. You can explain why. You can handle it well.

> 'Motivation is what gets you started.
> Habit is what keeps you going.'
> – Jim Rohn

Align actions with bigger plan/ objectives

Context is everything. This is a mantra I repeatedly say to leader-managers because an action taken in one situation with one person could well require quite a different action in a different situation. The danger with being myopic and inflexible is that the bigger plan or objective can be lost in a haze of busy action and good intention.

> 'Things which matter most must never be at
> the mercy of things which matter least.'
> – Johann Wolfgang von Goethe

Story: When I started working at one of the large Anglo-Dutch oil companies I had four department managers reporting to me. Two were staffed with small, tight numbers. The other two had bigger teams and a wider service remit. These latter also had massively higher sickness absence and staff turnover rates. My given remit was to reduce absence levels and headcount costs.

Common practice was to replace all leavers. A new procedure was established; to assess the service level agreement, team competence and budgetary versus actual staffing levels before making a decision. This frequently meant not replacing each person who left. Soon, in the biggest department (80 staff when I started), we reduced the staffing level to 73 and within 18 months it reduced to its optimum level of 62. The business imperative to improve service levels through training and engagement and to reduce costs was achieved.

Every absence required an interview with the operations manager (me or deputised rep). This was a massive commitment in time and energy, but it was worth it. The culture changed. Attitudes changed. Sickness absence reduced by 53% in six months. They attended work because staffing levels were tight; there was no one to cover for them and they didn't want to let their colleagues down (commitment and consistency again). We celebrated and acknowledged this with a huge poster in their office highlighting the improvements week by week, until it achieved its highest level at 97.9%. (A number of long-term sick employees prevented 100%.) It was a massive turnaround in culture, cost savings and in attitude.

This example is included because it shows not only what happens when actions align with more strategic plans and intentions, but also that achieving the ultimate goals can take time and effort and doesn't always go smoothly. I learned a great deal about working with department heads to change the culture, handling difficult conversations, putting formal disciplinary procedures into effect while managing the motivation of the teams at the same time. Sometimes it felt as if I was taking two steps forward, one step back. What mattered was that we had a clear vision of what we wanted to achieve for the division and we were prepared to be tenacious about it, despite the setbacks.

Communicate the why!

Most people coming into work have a good idea of what the day will hold and what they want to get done today. Some will stop and think about 'how' to get the task done quickly, or more efficiently. Some will think about 'who' they can allocate this task to so that they can get on with something else. And sometimes that works well.

Every employee worth their salt knows 'what' tasks to do and most employees know 'how' and 'when' to do their tasks. However, Simon Sinek says, 'Very few people and organizations can clearly articulate WHY they do what they do.' http://tinyurl.com/ q9go2oh

- When you share ***what*** needs to be done, you're allocating tasks

- When you explain ***how*** it needs to be done, you're either teaching them how because they don't know, or you're micro-managing if they do

- When you explain ***when*** it needs to be done you're prioritising and giving a deadline

- When you communicate the ***why*** you are sharing the drive behind the action; you're being clear about its importance and wider impact.

Frequently, the 'why' comes a late last, if at all. Not good.

'Because' is a magic word.

Once people around you understand the why, they begin to figure out how and when to do it for themselves. They can then adjust the speed and solve problems in such a way that it serves the 'why'. Explaining the why encourages people to get involved; it improves commitment to finding good solutions to problems and to finishing the task and, importantly, it makes people feel part of something bigger than themselves. They are not alone. They are contributing to something they probably couldn't or wouldn't achieve on their own. This is the real gift of the effective L-M. They generate real engagement, ownership and performance that people can take pride in.

Simon Sinek speaks about the importance of understanding and communicating the 'why' when you want to influence or inspire others. Watch Simon Sinek talk about a golden circle and the question 'Why?' How great leaders inspire action: http://tinyurl.com/o8jswn4

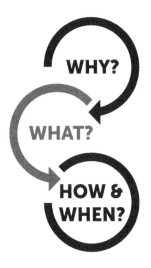

Fig. 15 Why, What, How, When?

It's more effective to first explain the why, then to discuss and agree the when, the how and the where.

When you fail to plan, you plan to fail.

Do your preparation

You've just read about being purposeful, the importance of communicating the why and anticipating various reactions. Here's a practice sheet you can use to think and plan before you act.

Issue / Topic / Problem:		
Who	What and Why	How You'll deal with it [say, do, ask, behave]
Person 1	Timing. They're under pressure to close off the contract.	
Person 2	Issues discussed at last meeting are still unresolved. Decision making is taking too long.	
Person 3	Client request to change specifications continue. This has implications for delivery, profitability and process.	
Person 1	Concerned about loss of key manager at a critical time. They rated her highly and their confidence in you delivering to time and cost is wobbling.	
Person 3	IT issues. It keeps failing and promised patches are not working.	

Fig 16 Doing your preparation

Avoid jumping into action too soon

Instant gratification: as a society, we're becoming addicted to it. You can order a book, online programmes, podcasts, and tutorials today. Many can be downloaded immediately by clicking on the link or, if it's a book, you can receive it from Amazon within 24 hours. You can check Netflix for your favourite movies, watch them now and not bother to wait a month until they show at the cinema.

Story: Recently, a manager called Steve told me he had an email from his boss at 9.20am and by 3pm he'd received two 'you haven't got back to me yet' emails even though Steve had said he needed to make some calls to ascertain the figures. He was working on gathering accurate info from others. He was determined not to 'jump to conclusions' because the data related to information that would go to an important client. His boss was clearly under pressure and wanting an instant reply.

Had Steve submitted inaccurate or incomplete figures it could have impacted the company's profitability in the long run. Also, he would surely have been in trouble when the inaccuracies were discovered. In this case, a mistake could have been costly, in terms of the client relationship, in terms of profitability, future business partnering opportunities and, importantly, the reputation of Steve's business in the eyes of the client.

Mistakes are often costly – people, process, profit

You know the value of planning and stopping to think before you act, yet at the same time, you feel under constant pressure to act, to decide, to argue the point. Then, often afterwards, when you reflect on what you said or did (or didn't say/do), you regret it. We regret our actions or words and we resent others who put that pressure on us.

Regret and resentment often go together. With that regret come defensiveness about the reasons and resentment with the person or situation that put you in this position. Sadly, the habit of jumping to conclusions/action too soon gets embedded and repeated. Resentments fester if not dealt with. Not good.

With the rise of technology and being 'online' 24 hours a day we can shop, arrange holidays, reply to emails, contribute to social media, and send outlook invitations and reminders at any time. This all reinforces the 'immediate gratification' drive we see around us. I'm not saying it's bad – it's not. It's wonderful, handy and useful *most of the time*. However, your job as a manager is to be aware of your tendency to jump into action too soon when you're feeling under pressure or impatient – and of others when they put you under pressure to act without thought.

So what's the answer?

It is NOT about *not* taking action; it IS about pausing, taking a breath while you consider what else/who else needs to be considered. Being a great fan of *Law & Order* on TV, I often think about this as 'doing my due diligence'. In order to make the right decision, in order to do the right thing. It's about taking high-quality action; about making good decisions; remembering to 'look before you leap'.

When the context is such that you're under fierce pressure to take immediate action, then your best option is to think fast and get advice when needed from experts.

Before you assume, learn. Before you judge,
understand. Before you hurt, feel.
Before you say, think.

In essence

- Never schedule back-to-back meetings. Always allow breathing and re-focus time

- Being busy isn't the same as being productive

- The antidote to busy-ness is focus on efficiency and effectiveness

- Schedule Outlook 'think and plan time', eg 'TPT 60', in your diary. Regularly

- Planning gives you time to understand and to prepare to succeed

- Do what you say you would when you said you would. If you can't, manage expectations and show courtesy to others

- Give yourself time to do your 'due diligence'. Take time to plan and prepare

- Use 'because' when communicating the 'why'.

CHAPTER 5

Understanding Resistance to Change

From resistance to acceptance

All change meets resistance ...
If there's no resistance, there's no change.

In this chapter you are invited to think about a couple of changes you've been through in the last year – they could be family, work, social, friendship circumstances. With these in mind, you can apply these principles to your experience ...

- Define resistance and understand why people resist change

- Discover where resistance is most prevalent in organisations

- Understand the five stages of resistance to change

- What people say and how L-M can respond

- Different types of resistance and how they show up

- Checklist for your change scenario

- Creating a climate of 'change acceptance'

- Explore how to address resistance

Defining Resistance

'Resistance to change is the action taken by individuals and groups when they perceive that a change that is occurring is a threat to them.'

The key words are 'perceive' and 'threat'. The threat need not be real or great for resistance to occur.

Another definition, from humanresources.about.com, is 'Resistance to change is the act of opposing or struggling with modifications or transformations that alter the status quo in the workplace'.

Resistance to change is easier to spot and less likely to happen in a culture of trust, transparency, engagement and honest communication. Employees who trust their line manager are much more likely to be willing and confident to discuss their ideas and worries openly. This helps smooth the change process and reduces the effects of unexpressed feelings and resentments which can sabotage the transition.

What does resistance tell you? It lets you know that others think and feel differently. It tells you they're not on board; it tells you there's more work to be done on engaging them; it tells you more listening and explaining the 'why' is needed; it lets you know they are afraid; it lets you know they need to know if they have choices – and if they do, what those choices are. It may also let you know where poor relationships between manager and employee exist, since a lack of trust and open communication can drastically impact the level and depth of resistance.

The more we are attached to a thought,
action, habit, process, person, the more
resistant we are likely to be.

One of the most common approaches to problem solving and
change I see L-Ms taking is how they treat change as a technical
process or intellectual exercise, when, in actual fact, it is also an
emotional process.

Jane's Story (pt 1): Jane took over as head of marketing
when Sarah, her boss, retired after 22 years in the role. Jane
had spent 12 years in the business, the last four as section leader
(deputy equivalent). She was ready, or so she thought. She had
dreamed about how she would be when she became head of
department; identified all the changes she wanted to make;
worked out just what her role would be; attended a robust and
challenging nine-month management development programme
to learn skills and develop insights into being a manager (as
opposed to an accountant turned marketing manager). She had a
clear vision of what she'd do, how she'd do it and a dream of how
it would be.

Intellectually, she knew there'd be resistance from a number of the
team; she knew who they were and felt confident she'd be able to
turn them around to her way of thinking.

Resistance and change are like two sides of the same coin. Lewin
describes what happens in teams and organisations during change
– the disruption, confusion, loss of focus and uncertainty, all of
which are examples of the resistance that comes with changes
before eventual clarity and re-settling.

In anticipation of a change of manager, for instance from Sarah
to Jane (as above), anticipation of an old manager leaving causes
anxiety, uncertainty and fear of what's coming; this disturbs the
status quo and generates questions about the future. When the new
manager comes online, the uncertainty continues about why some

were promoted and not others and speculation about who does what, how it gets done and why, etc, begins to happen.

Squabbling among the team is inevitable (as Tuckman's 'team stages' of storming comes into play). Petty jealousy and simmering resentments are often just beneath the surface. Competition between peers and team members for attention from, and credibility with, the new managers while norming takes place ... people changing responsibilities, people leaving ... till eventually a new reality settles on the team and they emerge into the stage of performing.

In teams that move through the early stages of change and resistance and get through it together, they arrive at a state where people know what they're doing and performance overall is quickly re-established. But it doesn't always happen that smoothly.

Jane's Story (pt 2): Much of Jane's preparation served her and her team well. However, it wasn't all plain sailing. One member of the team was given added responsibilities and a slightly larger area to work in and this created untold resentment.

Two of his peers started to play up, saying they would do tasks but not delivering. One, who had previously been very engaged and reliable, refused to take on simple new tasks and snapped at Jane when she asked for an update.

Over a period of about four months, productivity slowed down noticeably and the atmosphere in the team was clearly less friendly towards each other and towards customers. The effect of 'change' can be like the pebble thrown in the water; it causes ripples that are felt near and wide.

Where resistance most commonly occurs in the organisation

According to research by orgreadiness.com the commonly cited areas where resistance to change was found in organisations are as follows:

Middle managers	53%
Front line managers	19%
Senior managers	13%
Front line junior managers	7%
Executive and Director level	5%
All levels equally	3%

Ref: orgreadiness.com

Which level do you work at and do these stats resonate with your experience?

Recognising the forms of push back

Push back is another word for resistance, disagreement, reluctance, absence of understanding, opposition, divergent thinking. It may be caused by the topic or suggestion itself, or the push back may be a function of some other issue, such as a clash of personality, retaliation for an earlier argument or decision, or it may be evidence of (conscious or unconscious) powerlessness.

Sometimes, you'll be able to predict and anticipate push back. This is useful because it allows you to plan, a) how to avoid it in the first place or, b) how to handle it or, c) how to mitigate any damage the push back causes with others. At other times, it's more difficult to predict what it might be, where it might come from or why it emerges in the first place.

Forewarned is forearmed.

That is why 'thinking and planning' before you act is a great idea and will serve you well. This planning may well involve other stakeholders who can help inform and warn you of pertinent information. In itself, this too requires forethought and action; it requires presence of mind and commitment to doing the preparation that will ultimately drive better results when push back appears.

Push back comes in many forms most of which you'll be familiar with. Here's a reminder of what they are and questions you can answer in order to be prepared:

1. Reasoned argument:

- consider what the opposite and others' points of view are on the subject you're presenting; check whether their argument is founded on emotion, historical data, feelings, robust research, etc?

- be prepared to listen to establish what their key point is. Often the argument will be about part of the issue or suggestion, not the whole

- if their argument were to be about 'the principle' of the issue, how would you respond?

- if their argument were to be about 'the practice' or the practical point of view, how would you respond?

2. New or additional arguments that you hadn't considered:

- acknowledge the contribution of others

- ask them to expand on it, in the context of the current situation/discussion/debate

- be prepared that others may bring valid, reasoned argument – perhaps a perspective you hadn't known about

- consider how you can respond with respect and an open mind.

Since situations, context and priorities will differ each time, it's important to know how to express your response professionally and in a balanced way without assuming you or they are right or wrong … remember it may enhance, add to or deepen your point of view.

Here are examples of three different ways you might reply… (a 'yes', a 'tell me more' and a 'no')

1. 'Yes, that's a possibility I hadn't considered; sounds good. Let's kick the idea around right now.'

2. 'Tell me more about that and how it might benefit/challenge/improve/impact the current situation.'

3. 'Thanks for that. It isn't something I had considered because of the cost and time implications. It may be something we can use/do next time.'

Be sure to taste your words before
you spit them out.

3. Sceptic voices: tell yourself

- they have a different perspective to me

- they're sceptical for a reason (it could be a learned behaviour, practised over time, and nothing to do with me or what I'm saying)

- they may need time to reflect

- they may have a point. It's entirely possible we may never agree

- we may get to a time when they 'warm' to my idea if I can acknowledge their scepticism, show patience and demonstrate counter-evidence

- determine to speak to the issue not them as a person.

4. Habit:

- some people argue the toss just for the sake of it. They are not always aware of 'mismatching', saying the opposite; with them it is just habit

- others will offer poorly disguised opposition by saying 'I'm just playing devil's advocate'

- frame a couple of open questions to drill down to find out whether their point makes sense of not

- if not, prepare questions to bring to the surface what their reluctance, disagreement or fear is all about.

The skill with this one, if you know it's their habit to 'disagree', is to have the presence of mind to consider whether they have a valid point or not.

5. Being challenged (remember, being disagreed with isn't always a bad thing)

Everyone you meet knows stuff that you don't. This might feel like they disagree. They may disagree. They may not disagree — perhaps they're exploring, provoking, checking. This possibility is a useful thing to remember because being disagreed with isn't always about 'right and wrong'. Unless you think it is. It can be that they have a different experience, a different slant on the topic or solution; if they disagree with you it shows they have beliefs and the courage of their convictions.

Anticipating and accepting that everyone in the team doesn't think, feel and believe the same every time keeps the team and their thinking fresh; it encourages contributions and the richness of diverse points of view. If the atmosphere in your team is such that members can disagree without it being taken as a personal insult, or without sulking and defensiveness, it will encourage them to use their individual brains and collective wisdom in service of solution finding and issue resolution. $1 + 1 = > 2$

Acknowledge the challenge. Here are a few different examples:

'That's a good challenge; you're making us really think about the results we're likely to get if we take that action.'

'I can hear you disagree with what's been proposed. Tell us what your point of view is.'

'It's clear from everything we've been discussing that you are not happy about this business decision.' 'I've explained 'why' a number of times. Now, we need to move on with this meeting.' (Optional: 'Let's speak later if you wish, though I do want to let you know this decision is final – and your cooperation is appreciated.')

6. The Quiet Ones

In the run up to the parliamentary elections in the UK in May 2015, the press spoke about the 'quiet conservatives'. These were people who didn't shout about, or even share, their political affiliations in public.

Every team and group has quiet people. What's interesting is that the quietness can come from a range of reasons; from introversion, reflective style, lack of confidence through to boredom, being uninformed and lack of assertiveness. Avoid assuming it's any one thing. Quiet people often have plenty to contribute but for some reason either don't or won't engage in the debate/meeting. Consequently, they often go un-listened to and unheard.

This is where you come in. You can encourage them. For example:

'Sarah, I notice you haven't told us what you think about this.'

'Alex, will you share with the team what we were discussing yesterday about actions we can take?'

'Let's hear one different idea from everyone.'

'Thanks John, I noticed Ann made the same suggestion a couple of minutes ago. Ann, how about you expand … and John you can add to it.'

Three underlying types of resistance

Resistance lets you know you need to identify where the gaps are. Is it rational? Is it behavioural or interpersonal resistance? Is it emotional resistance? It can be helpful to decipher between them as a different approach may be needed for each one.

Type 1: Rational resistance

Pragmatism comes into play when new ideas, new pressures and changes are introduced into the working day. While the changes may seem logical and cost effective to some, others (often those who deliver the service or product) may have practical reasons for resisting the change in, for example, timing, budget available, sequence of work tasks, allocation of resources including people.

Potentially this is the easiest to resolve, by restabilising clarity of purpose, reasoned discussion and willingness to negotiate if necessary.

Type 2: Interpersonal resistance

This form of resistance happens in day-to-day life when, for instance, one person comes up with an idea and, because the person delivering the idea is perceived as a threat or is not respected or the information is confusing or incorrect, resistance in the form of disagreements and defensiveness arise and need to be dealt with. The skill here is to decipher whether it's the message or the messenger that's the central issue.

Type 3: Emotional resistance

If you hear someone (or yourself) saying something like, 'I don't know why, I just think it's a bad idea', this can be an indicator that the person hasn't articulated the real reason they disagree or are resistant. It can be a 'feeling', usually linked to an underlying emotion of, for example, fear of loss, jealousy, uncertainty, insecurity.

Emotional resistance can be conscious or unconscious – you may be quite clear what it's all about – or the real reason may be unknown to you and present more like a 'feeling', a sense or gut reaction. A couple of examples for emotional resistance include 'clash of personality' driven by jealousy, insecurity, fear of exposure, feelings of hurt, values clash. Emotional attachment to people, issues, tasks and location can also drive emotional resistance.

Historic resistance is usually based on something similar having happened in the past and because of the feelings attached to that event or series of events. It could be that in a previous similar situation you failed, were hurt or disappointed. Loyalty to colleagues, the company or previous boss/team can also cause people to resist changes. Managers often say they feel as if they're being disloyal to a former boss or colleagues if they 'like' the new boss.

It's also true that some emotional resistance can be a sound, gut instinct, not to be ignored. The important thing in this case is to get the person to share their thinking and experience and to have it listened to and considered in a fair and open-minded way.

Common reasons for resistance to change

Allied to the three types of resistance to change at work discussed above are covert or overt resistance at individual or collective level. Here's what to look out for:

'Dog with a bone' type of difference in opinion – high level of attachment, could be evidence based; intuition based; experience based; status based; or fear driven

Value clashes – some actions being taken may seem close to the unethical line for some employees. What is 'right and fair' can be perceived quite differently among employees. These value clashes may have cultural, generational, gender or experiential differences

Lack of trust in the manager – when this is the case between manager and employee, greater resistance, poor communication and low levels of engagement are inevitable

Practical issues – mobility, working patterns, role changes, security of tenure, allocation of tasks or benefits

Lack of employee involvement – if the changes have been presented as a *fait accompli* where no discussions or explanations have been forthcoming and where employees feel they have not been trusted with the truth, resistance will be greater

Different experience – someone who had a poor experience of a change/decision will likely be more resistant if similar future scenarios arise

Different goals – if the organisation is driving for goals in one direction and employees are driving for opposite goals there will be resistance

Perception of loss – in status, access to senior managers, income, future promotion opportunities, etc, as a result of the change

Fear of being wrong – strong attachment to the status quo is often a good thing – until it's time to change. Change can imply 'wrong' or 'not good enough' or 'inadequate' – and this elicits resistance and a defensiveness to maintain what is

Fear of being embarrassed – like shame, this is a painful feeling of humiliation or distress caused by doing or saying something that you or others think wrong or foolish

Fear for reputation – our perception of our standing in other people's eyes is important to most people – and if an organisation is implementing a change programme that challenges or belittles our sense of 'reputation' implicitly or explicitly, then resistance to change becomes inevitable – or the person leaves the business. Either way, it's a loss for the company.

Five stages of resistance to change

What we recognise now as 'The Five Stages of Change' is based on the work of Elizabeth Kübler-Ross, a Swiss psychiatrist who introduced the world to the phases of grief a dying person goes through. These are her Five Stages of Grief:

1. Denial: This cannot happen to me!

2. Anger: Why did this happen to me? Who's to blame for this?

3. Bargaining: Just let me live 'til my daughter's wedding, and I'll do anything.

4. Depression: I am too sad to do anything.

5. Acceptance: I'm at peace with what is coming.

In the business world

In the 1980s consultants in the business world began to notice parallels in employees' reactions to major change caused by the economic downturn and recession.

1. Shock: I can't believe what I'm hearing on the news!

2. Denial: This recession won't last long. We won't be let go. We'll weather the storm OK.

3. Anger: Why didn't the directors do something to stop this happening to us?

4. Depression: I'm so afraid. What will I do if I lose my job and can't pay the mortgage?

5. Adaptation: My new role isn't as interesting as the old one, but it might improve.

6. Acceptance: We have a good team – and we're now working with old and new clients. Things are looking up.

As you read on, you will likely recall noticing similar reactions to those explained by Kübler-Ross's model in yourself and other people confronted with redundancy, dismissal, enforced relocation, divorce, disability and injury, relationship break-up, and major organisational changes.

I made a note some years ago that Kübler-Ross never meant for the five stages to 'help sort messy emotions into neat packages'. As you'll know from your own experience and those around you, there's no one pathway through grief or major change. And although the five stages may look like an obvious sequence that we go through one at a time and in order, this is not necessarily true; we can move forwards and backwards many times and in different orders – and we may skip stages altogether, depending on the person, their resilience and the context.

In the image below you will see how our emotional-resistance response changes and shifts over time.

You can use the model to help you reflect on, and identify with, what's going on during major change. In this way you may be more capable of helping yourself and others 'weather the change' in the most constructive way possible.

Ref: Daryl R Connor, *Leading at the Edge of Chaos*

5 Stages of Resistance

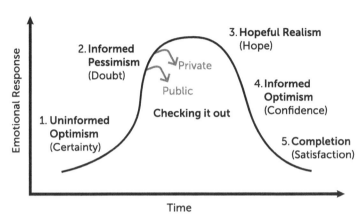

Fig. 17 5 Stages of resistance

Remember, people differ and their reactions differ – from each other and from context to context. We saw that quite clearly in the chapter about the three generations. Some people thrive on organisational change and a bit of chaos, while others struggle with it in one context but not in another. What I've learned is that people's reactions to change, trauma, uncertainty is never 100% predictable or uniform and it is frequently different from one situation to another. Without a doubt, it's a complicated subject when you scratch beneath the surface. We're not going to do that here, so I'm keeping this light touch.

In the real world, the five stages of resistance become apparent in many situations such as:

- Economic pressures, as we saw in the recent recession

- Mergers and acquisitions, takeovers

- Re-structuring

- Changes in significant leadership roles

- Threatened/actual redundancies

- Organisational change

- New joint venture partnerships and alliances

Here's an example of the effect of the recent global-local economic recession:

5 Stages of Resistance	Effects of Economic Recession This is what you may hear being said...
1. Uninformed optimism	"We're doing alright at the moment. Those politicians/ broadcasters always exaggerate. We've heard it all before. If it does happen the company will look after us. It'll be ok. People still need to build/to buy etc...what we do.
2. Informed pessimism	Hmmm. Business has slowed down. Some people will be made redundant after all. We have enough work to keep us going (public). I hope I won't lose my job (private). Keeping a close eye on what's happening.
3. Hopeful realism	The economists are saying things are picking up. I'm not seeing it, but it will hopefully show up.
4. Informed optimism	It's getting busy again. People are more optimistic and our clients are spending money again. It'll take us a while to get back to where we were, but we're on the up. Yeah!
5. Completion. New reality.	We'll learn the lessons of recession. Keep things lean and effective. Continue to control costs while working effectively – that way we'll be more profitable."

Fig. 18 5 Stages of resistance – worked example

Resistance to Change.

Issue:

Name	Context of Change	Individual (or group) issues	What's NB to them ?	Underlying reasons may be…
Alex and 2 peers	Unpopular line manager returns to manage team	• Temporary L-M is very popular • 'Old' L-M had obvious favourites and everyone knew who • 'Old' L-M returning means things go back to how they were (not good) • Work practices recently established may be rescinded • More upheaval	• Moving forward not backward • Fairness. Impact of favouritism if it continues • Working with a line manager they respect	• Anticipation of workplace not being such a happy place • Sense of unfair treatment for some team members in the past • Uncertainty about the future • Clash of values • Loyalty to temporary L-M
HR Team	New HR System	• Long held routines and methodologies • Workload increase anticipated • Lack of belief in the need for new IT system • Team animosity towards their line-manager	• Maintain status quo; routines and team norms • Security of employment • Not asked to do work they are not able to do • Feeling they can exert some power	• Comfort and confidence with current situation • Absence of buy-in to new changes • Fear they won't cope with new system • Ignorance of WIIFM • Absence of trust in line-manager • Ignorance that the change is not negotiable

Fig. 19 Exercise: Exploring who is resisting

Who is resisting?

As a manager you'll have either heard or given many of these reasons over the years. Sometimes they are real reasons; other times they are excuses. Here are a few of the best 'excuses' I've heard for not doing something. Then below, how they may be interpreted:

> I haven't had a chance yet
> He didn't turn up at the meeting
> I haven't managed to get round to it
> We had a rush job on. I'll do it next week
> Someone else was there and I couldn't
> I've tried this before and it didn't work
> I don't want to hurt/upset them

Excuses: an interpretation

Now, let's add an interpretation to these statements as excuses. Feel free to add any other interpretations you think of.

'Reason' given for not doing	Interpretation
I haven't had a chance yet	Risk averse Poor prioritising
He didn't turn up at the meeting	Relief Denial Convenience
I haven't managed to get round to it	Inertia Conscious or unconscious resistance
Someone else was there and I couldn't	Lack of commitment Using others as a distraction
I don't want to hurt her	Lack of commitment Fear of success
I've got to work the with guy	Fear of not being liked Low self-confidence
It's not the right time	Lack of ambition or courage
I haven't had time to plan / I don't have the resources/materials/ stuff	Lack of effort, commitment Lack of planning

They know they've done wrong, they don't need me to tell them	Collusion Denial of your responsibility
We had a rush job on. I'll do it next week	Dishonesty Uncommitted
I tried this before and it didn't work	Fear of failure Unwillingness to learn another way
I'm going on holiday /s/he's going on holiday for two weeks	Over optimistic Hope of escaping what should be the inevitable
I have so much else on	Disorganised Failure to prioritise

Fig 20 Reasons for 'not doing'

Ways to overcome your own excuses!

There can be a fine line in the difference between an excuse and a reason. The person giving it perceives it as a 'reason' while the other person will be the ultimate judge of whether it is a justified reason, or whether it's an excuse.

Leading by example is important for leader-managers, and with this in mind, you can reflect below on the 'reasons/excuses' listed and consider how you mentally deal with your own resistance.

In this way, you will lead by example. When you notice yourself using these types of phrases, do a mental check with yourself: 'Is this the truth, or is it an excuse?' If it's the truth, deal with it. If it's another excuse, having an alternative re-frame may well help you.

When other people offer poor excuses to you, it's common to assume the worst, to think judgmentally about them. This affects your state of wellbeing as you expend emotional energy in dealing with it.

Another way of looking at these is ...

'Reason' given for not doing	Alternative reframe
I haven't had a chance yet	I've bottled it so far. Today I will do it
He didn't turn up at the meeting	I'll pop round to see him to discuss the issue with him
I haven't managed to get round to it	I haven't prioritised this. Is it or is it not needed to be done ? Decide one way or another and act accordingly
Someone else was there and I couldn't	I failed to mention there's an issue needed and to find space in diary
I don't want to hurt her	It's my responsibility as a L-M to make people aware of... eg that her aggressive comments are not helping cooperative spirit in team
I've got to work the with guy	This is why I need to be honest with him
It's not the right time	If it's true, park it. If it isn't 'man up' and do the thing
I haven't had time to plan / I don't have the resources/materials/ stuff	I haven't made the time or arranged the resources. Time to own the decision
They know they've done wrong, they don't need me to tell them	It's my responsibility as a L-M to make people aware of... eg their under performance
We had a rush job on. I'll do it next week	Never put off till next week what you can do today
I tried this before and it didn't work	Learn how. Rehearse, practice. Gather your courage
I'm going on holiday /s/he's going on holiday for two weeks	Do it before. Be proactive and courageous. Something will change (hopefully improve) while you're away
I have so much else on	Really? How long will it take? 2 minutes? 10 minutes?

Fig. 21 Reasons for not doing – alternative reframe

Preparing to deal with resistance

When change is introduced it is wise to expect some level of resistance and reluctance. If you expect it, and you can assess the reasons for the resistance accurately, then you are halfway to dealing effectively with it and possibly even heading off the time-consuming and virus-like negativity that can come with significant resistance to change among employees.

Dealing with resistance is part of accelerating change acceptance. Acknowledging the resistance doesn't have to mean you agree with it. If members of the team or colleagues have their own reasons for worry, acknowledging it acknowledges their fear, their worry, their anxiety. This action, this reassurance, can sometimes be enough to allay their fears – and improve their readiness to accept inevitable changes.

Removing blockages can help in a practical way also. People in the organisation have ideas… they have experience, knowledge. Use ***their*** brains – engage them in the problem-solving at a level where they can contribute. Let them know what the goal is and task them to come up with local ways to contribute to the bigger target.

 Story: Engaging the Team in Change

Cost savings were being prioritised in one organisation I was working in during the recent recession. The finance director sent out an email to all senior managers directing them to cut costs in every department. I was working at the time with Tom, one of the departmental managers.

Instead of making decisions and communicating them to his team, Tom arranged for a team meeting. He explained the message and the urgency and asked for suggestions. In their local office hub one of his team calculated there were over 30 printers around the offices. They researched spending on printers, paper and toner cartridges. He then carried out research with the team regarding the minimum number of printers they could practically reduce down to. They agreed 23 – and later reduced to 19.

Savings amounted to several thousand pounds over six months, helped by their suggestion that they only print essential documents. This joint goal and effort was a small thing – yet it had a huge effect on team morale and continued engagement.

Tom's team were one of the least resistant and most effective over the lifetime of the recession, so his engagement of them and their continued involvement in problem-solving had a positive long-term effect.

Preparing to deal with resistance – ask and answer

As we discussed earlier, in chapter four (Think and Plan before You Act), dealing with inevitable resistance is more likely to be successful when you prepare in advance.

Here is a set of questions you can usefully ask and answer as part of your preparation:

Questionnaire: Do Your Prep Before You Launch Into Dealing With Resistance
How urgent is it that you engage with them? What's driving the urgency?
How will you communicate the 'why' of the change? How will you couch it so that it makes sense to them in the given context?
What level of trust and openness of two-way communication exists between you and your team/stakeholders/boss etc?
What damage control needs to be managed? What could the damage do if you don't deal with it?
What will the costs be if you do, what will the costs be if you don't? What costs won't be incurred if you deal with it? What costs won't be incurred if you don't deal with it?
What is negotiable in this context?
Where is there room to manoeuvre / room for flexibility within boundaries – what is negotiable or could be ? (based on business priorities)
What is not negotiable – it's a done deal?

What resources people and physical, are available to you / them to help them process the change ?
What is the optimum time and place of resistance conversations ? Is it wise to ask people to prepare for the conversation ? If so, what question/s would be helpful ?
What evidence is there of the need (the why?) for the change ? especially, what evidence or reason that will appeal most to them?)
What costs (people, profit, process) will be incurred?
Will you see people on a 1:1 basis, as a group first or visa versa ?
Who are the formal influencers? What position are they taking about the change (privately? publicly? – these may differ)
Who are the informal leaders who you need to get on-side if you possibly can? What position are they taking (privately? publicly? – these may differ)
What are the benefits of the change that people are resisting ? Who will benefit ?
Add Your Questions Here:

Fig. 22 Questionnaire: Do your prep

Twenty ways to create a climate of change acceptance

When change is non-negotiable, your job as a leader-manager, on behalf of the organisation, is to accelerate and support the move through change and resistance to acceptance and renewed effectiveness.

Here are proven ways that help:

- giving maximum warning of changes and implications, eg details and particulars of the change

- deal with objections (see below)

- speak in terms they understand; avoid jargon and unfamiliar technical expressions

- acknowledge concerns; be honest about what is and what is not possible or what is or isn't going to happen

- explaining the reasons (the 'why') in language they can understand and relate to

- remind yourself about the five stages of resistance so that you can accurately spot where people (and you) are

- share theories of 'change' such as those of Kurt Lewin and Elizabeth Kübler-Ross so that people understand the process and feelings that go along with change

- be clear about 'what's in it for them' – not just the organisation

- highlight the positive outcomes or consequences so that people have something positive to cling on to in tough times

- be clear about what's negotiable and what is not. Boundaries can create a sense of security

- involve people in planning and implementing; discuss SWOT of change

- manage expectations around uncertainty and how long it may continue

- be seen and heard around people in the business. Noticeable presence of senior management is incredibly important in uncertain times

- communicate over and over and over and over (even when there's nothing new)

- consider whether gradual or swift introduction will be more effective; either way, show quick results

- allow time for, and encourage, development of new skills

- be pragmatic about objections. Avoid thinking you'll overcome all objections. Each individual will ultimately choose one of the following responses:

- accept that people 1) will (ultimately) accept and stay; 2) won't accept and stay; 3) seem to accept yet leave the team or the organisation; 4) don't accept and leave

- remember that individuals are… individual

- check on how people are coping – support, reassure, excite, inspire as appropriate

> 'Success is the sum of small efforts,
> repeated day in and day out.'
> – Robert Collier

In essence

- Resistance is normal and to be expected. And yet, leader-managers across the globe resist acknowledging and dealing with it … until it escalates to such a point that there's no longer an option.

- Embrace it and deal with it. Facing up to it and finding tools to understand it will help you. Accurately anticipating it and dealing with it consistently at a local and global level across the organisation will reduce the fallout in terms of performance, retention, stress and, ultimately, commercial success.

- Exploring and understanding the difference between your own 'reasons' and 'excuses' can make all the difference to your performance as a leader-manager.

- Motivation, personal values and engagement are closely connected. Understanding the first two will help you achieve a high level of success in the third.

- If you can accurately gauge reasons for and levels of resistance to change, your actions to create a climate of acceptance for change will be more successful.

- Trust, employee engagement and open communication are key at all times but especially at times of change. In organisations and teams where trust and employee engagement are healthy, resistance to change can be a vehicle for open discussion and exploration of options for action; decisions can come from within and consequently minimise resistance. If it's the team's idea or they were involved in the strategising and thinking and understand the drivers for change, they are much more likely to buy into and support the change.

- Use this chapter, together with others in the book, to help you and your team and organisation face up to the resistance that comes as part of the package of change. It will be a much less scary and insurmountable challenge to tackle if you do.

CHAPTER 6

Managing Good Performance and Underperformance

'The art of conversation, like everything else,
can be cultivated. No one can expect to talk
well without practice.'
– John Lubbock

The level and consistency of employee performance is the difference between success and failure in any business. In order to achieve commercial results, employees need to be enabled to perform to their best. For this to happen, their performance needs to be proactively managed.

In this chapter I want to take you through a journey of understanding the why, what and how of managing performance. This will include: how to address underperformance in such a way that people engage with the conversation and the issue; what to avoid doing and saying when dealing with underperformance and the defensiveness that comes with it.

Let's start with a fundamental truth; the core purpose of managing performance is to achieve long-term goals and outstanding results. And the responsibility for managing performance is ... that of the manager. This means it is a manager's task to create a culture where all employees see themselves as a key part of the business and realise that their individual actions impact the success and growth of the business as a whole.

> **Story:** One of my current clients is a huge advocate of what I call 'tight performance management' (TPM). This means strict weekly/monthly/quarterly targets are set and monitored in every department. Status against targets is updated daily on whiteboards and on Trello, an interactive online communication and project management tool that can be made visible and accessible to everyone in the team. Individual and team tasks and goals are included – and it makes everything, including progress, visible. Major successes (when they outperform targets) of employees at every level are publicly celebrated. This drives the most amazing spirit in the whole team, from top to bottom; it has the effect of making every team member want to perform, want to do a great job and be willing to help others and to go the extra mile. The use of applications such as Trello and Beesy.me to share information across teams, across the site and with remote workers, can be a practical tool to engage individuals, monitor performance and highlight issues of non-compliance and underperformance as well as successes and positive achievements.

Some people might say this level of public visibility and accountability would be a nightmare. That may be true for some, but in the company, when things are going well, individuals and teams feel a huge sense of pride, of wanting to outperform their own performance. When things are not going so well, they are motivated to sort things out and get back on track. The culture of the company referred to above has changed significantly in the last ten years or so, due to the leader-manager, Simon, who came on board at that time. Even as a middle manager Simon was an advocate of 'tight performance management'. As his teams performed well consistently, he moved up the organisation, and his tight performance management (TPM) approach became more prevalent as other managers replicated his method.

At the same time, the culture doesn't shy away from failure to perform. Targets are set and when they are not achieved, this is dealt with head on. Managers discuss with the individual and the team. The approach is 'take responsibility for fixing it' rather than a blame culture. Root-cause analysis is widely used when appropriate, in addition to other problem-solving frameworks. Understanding 'the why' leads them to develop a tactical approach to resolving the issue and avoiding it recurring. It's not perfect; it doesn't always work. If one team member continues to underperform despite support from the team, they are moved to a role they can perform successfully (if one is available) or they exit the business. This is a great example of a company where managing performance (from great, to good, to under) is a business driver.

Failure to manage good and underperformance will have short-, medium- and long-term implications for the business as well as for the team. Where an absence of active management of underperformance occurs, the main culprit is the manager. That's where the buck stops. In effect, managers who fail in this respect are also failing to lead by example; they are, by omission, sending a message of 'acceptance of mediocrity' and effectively encouraging a culture that accepts poor levels of accountability.

Why manage performance effectively and confidently?

The responsibility of every leader-manager is to manage performance in two broad areas and to do so confidently:

1. **Promoting good performance** – through recognition, praise, encouragement, development and acknowledgment

and, when appropriate, through promotion or other opportunities

2. **Managing poor performance** – through discussion, clarifying expectations, restating standards, agreeing action and, when necessary, taking disciplinary action

Why? There are a number of really practical reasons every manager should manage performance properly and confidently.

One key reason is that the team know everyone is being held to account – this means they will know if you are not doing what you should – others are likely to try to get away with things too. Your credibility will suffer.

The second key reason, at a practical business level, is the need for leader-managers to be commercially aware. Applying the 'prevention is better than cure' principle, when you 'stop the rot' of poor performance and poor attitude, you save time spent in resolution, reduce mistakes, create a safer working environment, mitigate poor quality, prevent issues in the team from escalating, etc.

Other good reasons to manage performance *actively and confidently* include:

- employees know where they stand; there's a clear focus on what needs to be done and what's important; they work more effectively as a team

- demotivation and whinging are reduced ... fewer occurrences of sickness, absence, lateness, etc

- fewer misunderstandings about what is expected crop up and this reduces stress levels

- retention is improved; attrition is reduced and costs of spiralling turnover are curtailed

- productivity will improve

- and finally, it's your job; if you don't manage performance of the individuals in your team, who will?

Fact: Where underperformance is prevalent and persistent, the main culprit is the manager.

Here's another way to look at why managing performance is so essential to every leader-manager's practice.

The 8 Why's i.e. Purposes	The Question that the Performance measure can help answer
Evaluate	How well is my team/department/project performing?
Control	How can I ensure that my team are doing the right thing?
Budget	Is project funding being spent in the right area? Where should funds be spent?
Motivate	How can I motivate and sustain engagement of my key stakeholders? (incl my line-manager)
Promote	Who do I need to promote my team/department/project to? Who do we need to be visible and credible to?
Improve	What should we do differently to continuously improve performance?
Learn	What's working? What isn't working? Why? What do we need to repeat? What do we need to do differently?
Celebrate	What accomplishments are worthy of celebrating success? How can we best do this so as to embed a culture of effortless and regular appreciation?

Fig. 23 Why Managing performance is so important

Actively Promoting Good Performance

Recognition is a key success factor even at
higher levels of management.

The Why

> High performers are your greatest asset. Spend *more time* with them. Challenge them, stretch them.

One of your key tasks as a leader-manager is to manage good performance and to encourage high performers.

There are a myriad of ways you can actively manage good performance. Take a piece of paper and write a list of 10 things you can do right away.

10 things I can do right away to

Actively Promote Good Performance

1.
2.
3.
4.
5.
6.
7.
8.
9.
10.

Fig. 24 10 Things I can do right away

Your findings

How did you get on? Was it easy, tricky or difficult to come up with 10 things?

Many people will say recognition, praise, encouragement, development and acknowledgment, or other opportunities. You'll notice I haven't added 'salary increase' or 'promotion' to this list, as these are usually not something most managers can do right away or off their own bat. They are longer-term options.

Is this an exercise you can usefully do with your team? If so, here's an exercise you can take and explore with your team.

 Activity – Engaging Your Team.

This is a great activity to get your team involved. Bring along some A4 sheets printed with questions a) and b) (see below) and, having given a sheet to each team member, ask them to write a list of: a) what they can do to promote good performance throughout the team and b) what you can do to support them.

Compare your list to the list below of what to acknowledge – you may end up with a longer, more varied list that can remind you of easy, quick wins that have a great effect.

These questions are not only useful for the leader-manager to answer; everyone in the team has a perspective on this. Indeed, these questions would be equally useful when working with JV partners and in professional alliances. The shared answers may throw up invaluable ideas or suggestions; they may also bring unknown issues to the surface that can then be dealt with.

In managing good performance your key tasks as a leader-manager are to:

- Create a climate in which people want to do their best

- Motivate many kinds of direct reports and team or project members

- Assess each person's individual motivators and use them to get the best out of them

- Ensure that reviewing performance is not a 'one-off' event at PDP/appraisal time

- Reinforce values, results, effective teamwork, good performance, etc, on an ongoing basis.

Most managers intuitively know that recognition boosts our sense of wellbeing, our confidence and our ego. At the same time, they are reluctant, resistant or unconfident in giving recognition or praise. Some say it's because it might be misconstrued. Well, it might, but equally, when it's delivered correctly, it's much more likely to be taken at face value – and it makes the other person feel good.

Being on the receiving end of praise and recognition creates a chemical reaction in the body; we get a hormonal hit of serotonin – the naturally occurring 'happy hormone'. This has the effect of making us more optimistic; it can boost our motivation, our engagement – and frequently it renews commitment to the project, team, manager and even to the business itself.

Research: In 2004, the Gallup organisation conducted a worldwide research project, surveying more than four million employees about the importance of praise and recognition. Gallup concluded that employees who receive regular praise are more productive, engaged and more likely to stay with their organisation than those who do not. The survey results also indicated that employees who are praised receive higher loyalty and satisfaction scores from customers, and even enjoy better health than employees who are not.

'The Carrot Principle' presents the findings of a ten-year motivation study in which more than 200,000 employees and managers were interviewed. In their analysis of the results, authors Adrian Gostick and Chester Elton report that when managers are considered to be effective at 'recognising' their employees, they:

- have lower turnover rates than other managers

- achieve better organisational results

- are seen to be much stronger in goal-setting, communication, trust and accountability.

Actively promoting good performance

No one says that managing others is an easy option. The truth is, some of it is easy and some of it isn't. Being a leader-manager is a dynamic situation; one day is seldom like the next and every person you deal with is different from others. This is why behavioural flexibility and adaptability is an essential skill to develop and adapt. This is why being agile is such a benefit to leader-managers.

Responsibility for driving results and high performance **means**...

- Exerting your authority on behalf of the company. Your job is to achieve results through other people and that means being robust, fair and consistent

- Accountability – you are ultimately answerable for what you have been tasked to deliver

- Being agile in your approach – flexing the pace and process as appropriate, within boundaries of the law, ethics and procedures

- Understanding that behaviour breeds behaviour – if you behave respectfully under pressure, others are more likely to respond in kind

- Reinforcing what you want more of (not less). Acknowledge, praise and appreciate others

- Doing the right thing. Self-respect is something every leader-manager needs

- Motivating others to perform is part of your job. Coaching through demotivation is too

- Being prepared to tackle the difficult situations and difficult conversations through to resolution

- Bringing logic and honesty into play when performance is good and when it is poor

- Learning about people. Be part manager, coach, teacher, psychologist and friend

- If a person is underperforming persistently, it's because no one has called a halt to it

- Stepping up to the difficult conversations, even if no one else has in the past

- People will know where they stand with you (whether you manage underperformance or not)

- Some will like you; some won't. Some will like what you do; some won't. That's life.

The approach taken to managing performance (both praise and discipline) is representative of the culture of the organisation. A commercial manager I was working with recently commented that, *'the pendulum has swung from command and control management to laissez-faire. In the old days, the foreman ruled the roost. Now, most managers here pretty much avoid praising or disciplining. We're too soft. We need to find a way to achieve a better balance, where the culture is more accepting of managers actively managing performance and employees are more prepared to be held to account.'*

Taking action: praise/recognition v acknowledgement/appreciation

Here's something to think about. Are praise, recognition and acknowledgement pretty much the same thing? Or do they differ from each other? Can each be used for a different purpose?

Praise and rcognition: I find it useful to differentiate one from the other and to use them for different purposes. A manager can utilise praise and recognition to reinforce when someone has excelled; when action has been taken to overcome a tough challenge or a difficult situation. They work best when given at unexpected times, when the praise is quite specific to an outcome or output and used for more serious or impressive performance or attitude. They are best delivered publicly, so that the point, the message, is reinforced to all concerned. Look out later in the chapter for an elegant NICE process you can use.

Acknowledgement and appreciation: these can be useful in situations that are more informal; they can be light touch, often a little more generic than praise, and can be delivered publicly or privately.

The challenge for many managers in the UK and Ireland is that, unlike in the USA, we are much less prone to praising others, celebrating success, shouting thanks from the rooftops. That's OK in principle because we are who we are. At the same time, it's useful to understand the psychology of recognition (praising and acknowledging others). Here's how it works.

The psychology of recognition:

Managing good performance well requires awareness of the good work; if you don't notice it and understand the power that positive reinforcement can have, then you'll miss an opportunity to get more of it. It's easy to get so taken up by the busy-ness of working life that others' contributions are **beneath conscious awareness – unless there's a problem.** That's why, if you know you don't tend to notice good performance, you can go in search of it, in order to reinforce your approval of others' behaviour or results.

Some managers notice the good performance but don't believe it's their job to acknowledge, encourage or praise others – they're getting paid to do a job; why should they need praise or encouragement? For all the reasons below. Employees flourish under a positive spotlight; they – and we – respond well to a pat on the back because we all like to be respected and valued for our contributions.

> Employees who are supervised by highly engaged managers are 59% more likely to be engaged than those supervised by actively disengaged managers. – Gallup

There are two elements to giving recognition:

- the first is to notice, realise or identify the opportunity to recognise or acknowledge someone

- the second is actually doing something about it – giving the praise.

It takes a certain confidence and competence to praise and encourage *effectively* but that isn't a good enough reason not to do it. You see, there's a NICE formula (see later in the chapter) that you can use to good effect. It takes practice and persistence but you'll get good at it and then both you and your team will harvest the benefits.

> Surveys conducted by Sirota Consulting have revealed that only 51% of workers were satisfied with the recognition they received after a job well done.[1]

This figure is as conclusive as you could get – it has been reached from interviewing 2.5 *million* employees in 237 private, public and not-for-profit organisations in 89 countries around the world over a period of ten years to 2003.

Why recognition by manager (M) is important to employee (E)

(E) Good work from Employee = = >

    (M) Appreciation and approval = = >

        (M) Reinforces the value of the contribution = = >

            (E) Satisfaction and productivity rises = = >

                (E) Motivated to maintain or improve their good work

Fig. 25 Why recognition is important

If you'd like to read more about how power managers can engage, motivate and drive performance of their teams, read this http://www.gallup.com/businessjournal/183098/report-separates-great-managers-rest.aspx

Before you give praise or recognition consider this...

'People often say that motivation doesn't last. Well, neither does bathing – that's why we recommend it daily.'
– Zig Ziglar

Acknowledging others is part and parcel of the culture in some organisations; in others it's rarely done and when it is, it's received uncomfortably and people are suspicious of some hidden agenda.

Consequently it's worth spending time doing your preparation.

Doubtless it speaks to the wider culture in which we live and work, but many people feel uncomfortable giving and/or receiving positive feedback, praise and recognition and many managers rationalise not doing it because, 'I shouldn't have to praise someone for doing a good job – they're being paid to do it'. Equally, many people feel uncomfortable being acknowledged or receiving praise and in some people it generates distrust rather than pride. Sometimes 'trust' is at the core of the issue. If they trust the person giving the recognition, they're more likely to be able to handle it positively – and vice versa.

At the same time, given the 'generational changes' we discussed in Chapter 1, praise and recognition are needed more/expected by Generation Y. This reinforces the point of considering who it is you wish to praise and how they would most likely be able to 'hear' it. Match your style of delivery with their readiness for praise, performance, task allocation.

Systematic Approach

If you want to take a systematic approach to giving praise and acknowledgment, it can be helpful to reflect on the person, or on each person from a team, and consider it from the joint perspectives of skill and will.

- Is the person you have in mind well skilled or low in skill(s)?

- Is the person you have in mind highly motivated or low in motivation?

Note that you can apply these questions generally to their approach and performance or more specifically to an area of their work.

If we put this into a matrix format, this is what it looks like:

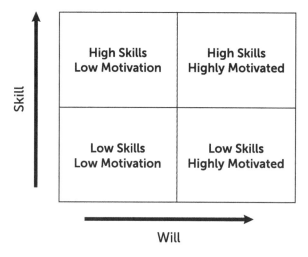

Fig. 26 Skill-Will Matrix

Now, answer these questions and they will give you a good insight into what you can acknowledge, praise and encourage – and what needs to be developed. Win-win.

Skill

- *What is the individual's technical ability in the role?*

- *What is the level of their other necessary skills and knowledge?*

- *What do they know and do well that deserves acknowledgement?*

- *Where have they gone the extra mile?*

- *Where have they made efforts to improve and pulled it off?*

Will

- *What is their level of willingness and motivation to carry out the wide range of tasks required in the role?*

- *Do they demonstrate a positive attitude?*

- *To what extent can you rely on them to do what they've been asked to do or what they say they will?*

When you identify levels of skill and will and gather examples, you have something specific to discuss with each individual and give feedback on.

Examples of what to acknowledge

- going the extra mile (showing commitment)

- stopping an issue before it becomes a problem

- saving time/money/resources

- grace under pressure

- creative solution finding

- commercial savvy-ness

- loyalty to the team, project, business

- consistency in results

- dependability

- high-quality decision making

- leading by example, eg safety, honesty, integrity, etc

- doing more than asked

- doing the right thing

- giving early warning of something going wrong

- significant improvement

If you focus on weaknesses, you doom
the worker to perpetual and impossible
self-improvement plans.

Reference http://happierhuman.com/benefits-of-gratitude/

Delivering praise, recognition, appreciation

There is a great deal of research to suggest that praising employees at work can be beneficial. However, the way in which the praise is delivered has a significant bearing on its effectiveness. Your job when giving recognition is to be specific about what they have done or said that has been appreciated and the reason why.

Here's an easy way to give recognition and praise by being NICE.

NICE Recognition/Praise

Follow the NICE steps listed when giving praise and encouragement.

N **Note the behaviours**, attitudes and actions you want to re-enforce positively.

I **Individualise it** – make it personal to what they did. Use their name.

C **Clearly state** what you wish to praise, acknowledge – be specific and be genuine; give details. Avoid bland and generic statements.

E **Explain the benefits** of their actions to themselves. Say why it's important to you, how it's of value to the team or business. Be sincere in your thanks. Remember to smile.

Then go away. This allows them to bask in the appreciation and how good it feels.

'What's absolutely critical ... is that the organization celebrates success. Those who perform must be recognized. Their behaviour and its results must be reinforced ... Managers have emphasized this point to me time and time again, suggesting that, as basic as it is, it is violated often enough to become an execution problem ... Give positive feedback to those responsible for execution success and making strategy work.'[2]

[2. Hrebiniak, Lawrence G. *Making strategy work: leading effective execution and change.* Upper Saddle River, New Jersey: Pearson Education, Inc., publishing as Wharton School Publishing, 2005, pp. 200-201. Dr Lawrence Hrebiniak, Professor of Management in the Wharton School at the University of Pennsylvania

Setting people up for performance success

In a similar vein as recognising good performance, behaviour and attitude, you can do yourself and everyone else a favour if you 'start as you mean to go on and start with the end in mind'. This means setting up your team, colleagues, clients, suppliers and colleagues for success by ensuring the following happens.

1. **Clear Expectations** – You can set people up for success by ensuring both you and they have a shared knowledge of what they are being depended on to do and what their role and responsibilities are in the business, and, importantly, they need to understand the impact of their actions or inactions.

   If people are not crystal clear about what is expected of them – and why it is expected – disparities in performance and behaviour are inevitable. If they don't feel able to come to discuss possible areas of confusion or disparity in understanding – or to re-negotiate as things change – then you have failed in this task.

   > In managing expectations ... you must make clear, and they must understand, the impact of their actions or inactions.

2. **Agreed Behaviours** – Sometimes people don't know where the boundaries are regarding what's OK and what isn't in the workplace. It is not always clear. An example of where this shows up may be in the different generations. What's acceptable behaviour to Gen Y is often quite different to Baby Boomers. Your task as a manager is to be consistent across the team (and the generations). The goal is to identify and clearly communicate what is acceptable and what isn't. This will ensure that everyone behaves in a way that cultivates constructive and positive working relationships.

3. **Measurement** – this is all about ensuring that the business and the individuals are achieving what is necessary to carry the business forward. If you have financial targets to achieve, then knowing where you are in terms of achieving the target requires measurement. As the old saying goes, 'What gets measured gets done.' If team members know they are being measured against agreed goals, targets, results, they can monitor and regulate their own performance. This is all part of managing expectations. Part of the measurement is

having a consistent approach for improvement if and when performance falls beneath acceptable standards.

4. **Gathering Evidence** – If you're managing a team it's unlikely that you'll be with the team every hour or even every day. In fact, virtual and geographically spread teams, often doing different shifts, have become the norm. This means you will need to involve others, inside and outside the team, in your gap analysis. Remember, your job is to gather facts not opinions as far as possible.

It is wise, in order to conduct a fair and accurate process, to review good as well as poor performance. Robust evidence gathering from people who were involved first hand will help you get to the root cause and ultimately aid good quality decisions. When things go wrong, there's seldom just one root cause. Find the causes and deal with them and you'll achieve your aim of setting people up for success rather than for failure.

5. **Development** – Without development opportunities for individuals, there is no chance for improvement. This can include all the usual forms of development such as attending company training programmes, being tasked to carry out a demanding 'stretch' assignment or learning new skills in the job. It can also mean gaining experience and knowledge in other parts of the company; becoming adept with new equipment and technology; taking on special projects alone or with colleagues; standing in for you or other senior people as appropriate, to expand knowledge, skills, competence and confidence of the person being developed. Recognition and acknowledgment of this growth by senior people can aid retention.

Every business is in business to achieve the goals and objectives they set for themselves. Commercial success is all part of business success; after all, every business wants to be able to maintain and sustain itself over time; to continue to employ its staff and contribute to industry. Each of these activities that set people up for performance success are practical ways you as a manager can contribute to your company's success – and to your own reputation as an effective manager.

Managing underperformance

In this section we'll explore:

- Purpose of managing underperformance

- Diagnosing underperformance

- Examples of underperformance

- Occasional/temporary v persistent poor performance

- Four reasons for underperformance

Note re underperformance and poor performance: Because some of my clients call it 'underperformance' and others refer to it as 'poor performance' I switch between these uses throughout. They are interchangeable, not indications of degree or levels of performance.

Purpose of managing underperformance

Unfortunately, performance management is seen as an unwelcome activity by many leader-managers. In particular it is unwelcome where expectations have not been communicated and if confrontation is perceived as likely when addressing the underperformance.

If someone were to ask you, 'What's the purpose of having a company disciplinary procedure?' what would you say? This statement from well-known civil engineering company BAM Nuttall expresses the purpose perfectly.

Maintenance of discipline is the responsibility of managerial staff at all levels. If minor disciplinary offences are overlooked, an opportunity to redirect an employee's attitude or behaviour may be lost. Additionally, overlooking an opportunity at an early stage may result in the situation escalating, leading to the need for more serious disciplinary action later. Bam Nuttall policy (used with permission)

Performance management drives employee behaviour to align with organisational goals and objectives. This alignment happens because (1) job responsibilities and expectations are clear and result in increased individual and team productivity, and (2) better information is available to use for compensation and promotion decisions.

Managers hesitate to provide candid feedback and have honest discussions with their employees and often fail to take action; if an issue is addressed early it can be prevented from escalating or from being repeated by other team members.

> Not to act on poor performance is to, in effect, accept and reinforce it.

In their CIPD textbook (ref below), Armstrong and Baron define performance management as 'a process which contributes to the effective management of individuals and teams in order to achieve high levels of organisational performance. As such, it establishes shared understanding about what is to be achieved and an approach to leading and developing people which will ensure that it is achieved'.

According to the CIPD, Performance management should incorporate:

- **Managing behaviour and attitude** – ensuring that individuals are encouraged to behave in a way that enables levels of performance to be achieved and fosters better working relationships.

- **Performance improvement** – throughout the organisation, in respect of individual, team and organisational effectiveness.

- **Development** – unless there is continuous development of individuals and teams, performance will not improve

Ref http://www.cipd.co.uk/hr-resources/factsheets/performance-management-overview.aspx

What is underperformance?

Accurate diagnosis of the root cause of underperformance is important and this is something managers can find tricky. Predictably, incorrect diagnoses can lead to problems such as wasted time, wasted effort, resentment and potentially escalation of the underperformance issue.

A different kind of acknowledgment to that discussed earlier is needed in order to manage underperformance. Once acknowledged, courage to face the potential confrontation is needed in order to resolve the issue and deal with the consequences.

You cannot change what you
don't acknowledge.

Is it occasional or persistent underperformance?

Before you can fix underperformance, you have to understand its cause. Does it come from lack of ability, unclear instruction, lack of resources or low motivation? Occasional underperformance may go under the radar because it is occasional. Perhaps it relates to one part of the job, one task or one set of skills.

Persistent underperformance is usually much more obvious and noticeable because it happens again and again, over time.

Both need to be addressed by the manager, otherwise they are likely to continue and may escalate or lead to more serious issues. The approach used to deal with them is essentially the same. The context, the outcome and the severity, of course, may well differ.

Story: Andy is a health and safety manager. He's been in role for over two years. He's generally a very good H&S manager, is motivated about his role and does a very good job. As part of his role, Andy compiles stats, and reports to and presents to the senior board every six months. At the first two meetings he was very nervous, he stumbled, got confused and generally didn't do a terribly good job. Everyone put it down to nerves and he was encouraged by his boss to attend a presentation course. However, although it improved it wasn't enough. Last month at an in-company international H&S Conference he was asked to present to and debate with his international peers. It was a nightmare. His nerves got the better of him; he gobbled his words; he spoke incoherently; he failed to make the impact needed to get the UK regional funding they were looking for and his reputation was shredded.

Q. Is Andy's performance persistent or occasional? How would you tackle this situation with Andy? What would help most to 'get him into his stride'; to re-build and sustain his confidence and competence in a conference context?

A. Write notes here on what approach you would take:

Common examples of underperformance
Attitude and behavioural examples

- Task not completed on time/to quality

- Lack of care with IT and other equipment or resources

- Absence trend

- Rudeness/aggressiveness toward colleagues, customers, contractors

- Lack of communication; not disclosing important information

- Not reporting things gone/going wrong

- Dishonesty; not admitting errors/mistakes or sabotaging others

- Divulging inappropriate information to other parties

- Whinging, moaning, negative attitude or approach

- Aggressive behaviour

- Not being a team player

Technical

- Incomplete or inaccurate reporting of stats/information

- Failure to respond to customer queries in a standard way

- Not working at quality/speed/quantity of production as required

- Failure to hand over to colleagues and peers covering

- Decision making that delays, disrupts or interferes with production process

- Providing inaccurate rates, estimates or quotes for tender documents or to clients

- Inaccurate charging for services provided

- Failure to control costs, quality standards, safety procedures

- Poor/no reason for failing to work to the programme – time, quality, costs

Four reasons for underperformance are shown below. This relates to some extent to the Skill-Will Matrix; it also offers two further reasons, both of which are worth considering before you take action.

Reasons for Underperformance

Don't understand
Not Clarified
Assumptions being made
Low confidence

Don't know
Absence of Knowledge
Standards, what good looks like Data, know how

Can't do
Lack of Skills
competence
Absence of Resources
people, info, money

Won't do
Unmotivated/ Demotivated
what is in it for me?
Environment
culture, other people's priorities,
Attitudes to risk previous experience

Don't assume "won't do" without checking the others.

Fig. 27 Four reasons for underperformance

3-7 Guided Pathway to Courageous Conversations

In the chapter (add number) on Handling Difficult Conversations, I introduce you to a 3-stage 7-step process which gives you a pathway that can be helpful in conversations that are difficult to handle such as poor attitude, instances of poor performance, more frequent mistakes, demotivation, when errors/accidents happen, etc.

These conversations frequently go off-course because of defensiveness, aggression, embarrassment and frustration. The 7-step pathway gives you a path to follow and allows you to go with the flow of the conversation while staying on the path, eventually coming to some kind of resolution or way forward.

Skill-Will

The Skill-Will Matrix was introduced earlier in the book. Now it's time to consider what approach to take once you've established where the person is in relation to skill-will.

As always, a different approach should be deployed, dependent on the need and context. Consider how best to use the approach highlighted in blue for the different scenarios you face.

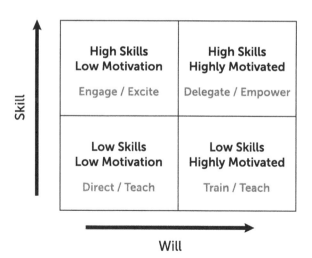

Fig. 28 Skill-Will and Approach Matrix

It is common to come across people in organisations with low or inadequate skills. Often, because they have done one job, it's assumed they can take on other tasks or a wider-scope job without ascertaining their real level of skill. Sometimes their low skill level is known and acknowledged and there's an intention that they'll pick it up as they go along. Some do. Some don't.

Another reason that people are low in skill is that technology, systems and role competencies have changed over time and the person's ability and confidence hasn't kept pace. Some will have the capacity to become sufficiently skilled; some won't. This is a conversation for the manager and the individual – and ultimately, it's the manager's decision, taken on behalf of the business.

Low ability may be associated with the following:

- Low individual aptitude, skill and knowledge

- Overly difficult tasks

- Evidence of strong effort, despite poor performance

- Lack of improvement over time

People with low ability may have been poorly matched with jobs in the first place. They may have been promoted to a position that's too demanding for them. Or maybe they no longer have the support that previously helped them to perform well. It's possible that what is required of the person in that job now is different from what was required when they were allocated the role or recruited to it. It comes down to capability.

Managing performance is a core business function.

Sometimes even after you have provided training, coaching, teaching and opportunity, performance is still not adequate. This is when leadership comes into its own. As a manager, you must act, because there are consequences to retaining an underperformer when nothing else has worked, for example:

- You'll annoy other members of your team, who may have to work harder to 'carry' the underperformer

- You'll give the unspoken message to others that you're prepared to accept mediocrity – or, worse, underperformance

- You may waste precious time and resources that could be better used elsewhere and cause delays, re-work or duplication

- You may signal that some employees deserve preferential treatment

- You will fail in your duty to manage performance on behalf of the business

Useful skills for managing performance

Core skills used in this context are similar to those being used in many other interpersonal interventions made by a leader-manager. What will differ is the context and the interplay between the parties involved.

In the early stages when underperformance has just begun, a lighter touch approach and more gentle tone of voice will be more typical than in later stages when repetitive discussions about underperformance have taken place. Effective leader-managers will escalate the formality of their approach and tone if sustained improved performance is not delivered.

Skills	
Observant listening	This means paying attention not only to what you hear, but to how it's being said; what is not said or avoided and to that attendant body language.
Questioning techniques to probe, challenge and clarify	Using mostly open questions such as What, How and Tell me about to probe beneath the surface. Use closed questions to hone in and to close.
Taking a coaching approach to engage (when appropriate)	It's useful to learn a structure for coaching conversations, such as IDEA or GROW. This will help you open up, explore, then close the interaction.
Clarifying assertively	Using comments such as "So what you're saying is..." or "Am I right in thinking that..."
Understanding what motivates the person	Take care about making assumptions about what motivates others. Check it out for yourself. It's often not what motivates you.
Knowing when to take a strict, disciplined approach*	When the issue is a serious one; when history suggests non-compliance; when other approaches have failed. Develop a range of responses, not just a couple of old favourites.
Giving feedback so it lands well	Adapt the content and approach so that it best lands with the person involved.
Setting objectives for clarity – and agreeing KPIs	Set goals that can and must be delivered. Inform consequences of non-compliance. Agree accountability.
Summarising effectively	Great skills to acquire and use. Shows listening, offers an opportunity to hesitate, consolidate. Can help you shift the conversation on, or back to where it needs to be.
Holding you and others to account afterwards	When under performance is evident and commitments are made between team member and manager, holding people to their word; being dependable is key to credibility. Agree not only what actions will be taken, but how they will be monitored and accounted for.
Consequence management	Can be perceived as aggressive or assertive, depending on how it is delivered. It's essential that an underperforming individual is made clear what the consequences of action and inaction and of complete and incomplete action. Get the team member to reflect back their understanding of consequences.

* this will relate to more persistent, serious cases

Fig. 29 Useful skills for managing performance

Ten top tips for managing underperformance

A few years ago I was asked by one of my clients to design, develop and facilitate a workshop aimed at building the knowledge, awareness and skills of managers throughout the organisation. One day I sat down with their senior HR manager and together we developed a list of 'top tips'. Thanks go to Jane Rostant. Here's a version of what we developed.

1. Separate poor performance from disciplinary issues. They are distinct. Deal with each appropriately according to company practices.

2. Limit performance management discussions to one or two performance issues at a time. More than that will confuse or prompt resistance.

3. Encourage individuals to develop their own ideas for improvement and enhancement of strengths. Ownership can be the difference that makes them take action.

4. Be firm and specific with an individual if you genuinely think there is a problem with their performance and they disagree. Give clear, relevant and current evidence/examples.

5. Give feedback about behaviour that can be changed or skills that can be improved, not about aspects of personality.

6. If the individual thinks there was no benefit to them in the progress review, it has failed. Find the benefit for them (even if this leads to consequence management).

7. Be prepared. Improving performance does not just happen … you need to manage both it and them actively.

8. Potential causes of poor performance? Lack of information, lack of skill, poor equipment, lack of motivation – don't assume it is the last until you have checked the others.

9. As a manager check that you can deliver (on training, new resources, change of location) for the individual before you promise something.

10. Individuals need to be involved in setting their own goals. The manager's job is to ensure they are relevant, stretching but realistic for that individual and provide the basis for success.

In essence

- Reinforcing positive and proactive performance increases employees' sense of being valued and aids retention

- The leader-manager's state of engagement influences the engagement and retention of employees

- Use the NICE approach when giving acknowledgment and praise

- Collect evidence of Skill-Will, etc, before managing performance. Get to the root cause (not just the symptoms)

- Distinguish between persistent and occasional (or temporary) underperformance and deal accordingly

- Call in HR for help with best approach, company policy, etc

- You can unlock the power of development and motivation by taking control and taking action

CHAPTER 7

How to Be an Effective Leader-Manager

Understanding yourself and how you can best contribute

What we're talking about in this book are people managers who are leading and managing day in day out, week in week out. They are dealing with employee issues, client challenges and changing business demands that develop and stretch those involved, in tandem with contributing essential technical input to the business.

It is likely you are a 'technical' expert and that you manage and lead; if you wish to be more successful there are a series of approaches, underlying principles and a few techniques that will be helpful to understand and use.

Q. What helps?

A. Understanding what's expected of you, by you and by others in your leader-manager role.

This applies to you irrespective of level of seniority. Get clear by being clear with yourself and others. Start as you mean to go on. If you are not clear, and others are not clear what is expected of you, confusion and conflict may result. Clarity may happen by osmosis, but it's a high-risk strategy in the short, medium and long term. In the absence of clarity, both you and they will 'make it up as you go along' and this becomes the 'story we tell ourselves' about what's expected. This is a recipe for disaster, as the 'stories' are never the same – and often meaningfully different. This could put you on a collision course with them, or them with you.

It's your job and your responsibility as people manager to educate others – in role and responsibilities; acceptable behaviours; where the boundaries lie; what you expect of them and what they can expect from you; consequences – of success and of failure.

(You'll read more about why and how to manage expectations later in the book.)

Q. What helps?

A. Not expecting to be all things to all people

No doubt you will know from your experience at work that different people want and expect a wide range of things from you. In one context this can be fine; in another it may cause you to feel pulled from pillar to post trying to satisfy them all. Directors and employees at all levels experience this.

Equally, it could be that you paddle your own canoe and leave them to expect the unexpected from you. Their expectations of you may include: anything they think the job entails; what's written in the job description; what's not written down but is 'obvious'; how the last person did the job/task, i.e. historical practices; personal agendas; unfulfilled promises; career ambitions; petty jealousies and just plain naivety.

The one thing to be aware of is that you can't be all things to all people. Ari knows this (see Ari's story below). Accepting this is simple in principle. In practice it can be difficult unless you know and clearly agree your lines of responsibilities, others' responsibilities, where you have agreed to differ – and how these differences get handled. You'll also need to agree a method of ongoing communication and adaptation while things bed down.

> Do your part to drive performance through people to achieve business objectives and company values.

There are times when you must accept that people will expect things of you that you can't deliver. The more senior you are, the more this is true I believe. Accept it and do whatever is practical to mitigate the consequences. And remember, you don't have to do it all yourself; get peers and other senior managers to communicate and engage on your behalf.

Ari's Story: I coached a sales manager who, after three years in the role, achieved the most successful sales figures for new cars across the network. This was a significant achievement.

However, his start in the role was unusual. Ari loved the detail; was a stickler for knowing and following to the letter every part of the company sales process – and they had processes for everything. When he joined the company he spent the first three months getting to know every aspect of the roles of his direct reports. He oversaw virtually every customer meeting, signed off every sale, was at the handover of every car; his team said he did more of their job than he did his own. Soon he became known as a 'control freak' and his team said, 'He doesn't trust us to do our jobs'. As soon as he realised his single-mindedness was impacting the team negatively, he flexed his style (just enough).

Knowing the detail of their roles and their sales process gave him a level of insight into where changes/improvements were necessary; he studied his team and quickly grasped the strengths and areas for development of the individuals in his team, where training was needed, where confidence needed boosting.

By his approach, Ari proved he was a superior sales person, willing to continually learn and skilled at dealing with difficult customers – so his credibility in his team soared. Over time, he made changes and brought the team along with him. Discretionary effort increased, upselling increased to a level never seen before in that dealership, and attrition of staff fell from 55% to 39% in 14 months. He's one to watch; no doubt he'll be a general manager of a dealership within the next few years.

It may be disappointing to realise that not everyone will like you. It helps to accept that, no matter how hard you try or how much you want everyone to know, like and trust you. They'll have their own reasons, some of which will be rational and comprehensible; other reasons will be irrational and incomprehensible. The best you can do is find a way to do what needs to be done in alignment with doing your part to drive performance through people to achieve business objectives and company values.

The most common time for managers to be taken advantage of is in their first six to nine months. New leader-managers are under pressure to prove themselves. They are usually keen to hit the ground running; to get up to speed quickly with people, processes, challenges and priorities. Some are so keen to make a good impression that they may be perceived as overly agreeable to the extent that they can be perceived as a soft touch; others want to exert their authority. As in so many areas we'll look at here, balance is the key. Knowing you can't be all things to all people any of the time is an important lesson to learn – and having the skills to deal with the consequences is essential if you wish to set the scene for a successful career in leadership and management.

Q. What helps?

A. Remembering to apply gap analysis

As you will no doubt know, even the most experienced and settled team has gaps in performance, skill, behaviour or attitude. If you consider this a given, you're much more likely to be on the watch for it and to spot it early on. Leader-managers who think their team is completely satisfactory are less likely to notice gaps, and if they don't notice the gaps, they won't deal with and resolve the consequences.

The final paragraph of Ari's story shows one way he went about understanding his team, so that he could accurately identify what the gaps were and take action to fill those gaps. The effect this had on his team was to build the general competence of the team and, with that, their confidence. All boats rise with the tide; in this case, Ari's commitment to up-skilling his team was the tide.

In terms of how to conduct a gap analysis there are a myriad tools and techniques available to you. Just do an internet search. A SWOT analysis is a simple format and useful for determining the strengths, weaknesses, opportunities and threats of ideas, actions and opportunities. The purpose of the SWOT analysis is to help you plan forward by using strengths and opportunities to overcome weaknesses and threats.

In contrast, root cause analysis (RCA), when conducted properly, is much more detailed and rigorous and is most commonly used to identify the underlying causes of why an incident occurred (or continued to occur). This may be a relative disaster such as safety, commercial, quality, etc. The purpose of RCA is to accurately define the cause of the problem so as to be able to address the root cause and avoid repetition of the problem in the future. Here's an example of exploring the root cause of a *very* simple issue. More often there are multiple answers at all levels.

> RCA: the objective of the exercise is to get to
> the truth of the root cause so that the solution
> is lasting and cost effective.

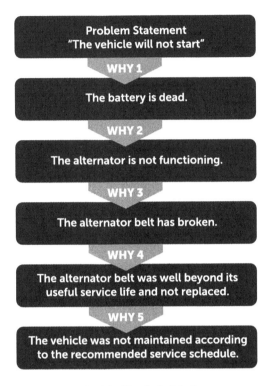

Fig. 30 Simple 5 Why's

Conducting a root cause analysis is a thoroughly fascinating and insightful process. Best done thoroughly and in a location with plenty of white wall space (with flipcharts and pens), it is a vastly underutilised tool across industry. Criteria for success are: time; knowledge of the context; an open mind; patience; detail orientation; willingness to keep drilling down; lateral thinking and ability to notice themes. In particular, it works best when those exploring it work with 'no attachment to the answer'.

Remember, the objective of the exercise is to get to the truth of the root cause, not to vindicate your or someone else's actions – and certainly, it's not about going till you get the answer you want. **Warning:** to get to the real root cause does take time and effort – and the ability not to jump to solutions or assumptions as you go along. Sometimes there are what look to be root causes, but often there's more beneath. Work on the principle that there's more to uncover than you have found so far. Be tenacious and patient. Be thorough. It will be worthwhile!

Q. What helps?

A. Agile managing

I like this word 'agile'. It means dexterous, light-footed, quick, deft, supple. Leader-managers who demonstrate agility of mind and behaviour will surely conquer opportunities and challenges presented more confidently and more effectively than those who do not.

The workplace and the work we do are constantly changing. Sometimes you may be in the same role for years, yet the challenges and work are quite different from one phase to another. When you begin a new project, even if the team is the same or largely the same, the project is different, the goals will shift, the challenges will be different and the contributions people make will change.

Whether you've been promoted or are doing a different project in a new context, how well you establish your style and solidify your ongoing approach has the potential to make a significant difference to the following:

- Ultimate success or failure of the project
- Employee engagement
- Grasping strategic and operational data, processes and procedures
- Performance of individuals
- Relationships with clients
- Financial success and business growth
- Cooperation with peers, colleagues

- Strategic direction and potential expansion

- Capacity of those delivering to deliver on time, on budget, to specification

– Being an agile leader-manager means thinking about how you behave, how you approach easy and difficult things and people, noticing the effect it's having and being deft in flexing, when necessary, to achieve the wanted outcome

– it means thinking about what strengths you have in your organisation (or team) and where these strengths can be best employed (irrespective of the job role)

– it means identifying where the gaps are – in knowledge, experience, behaviour, attitude, engagement, contribution, etc, and then filling those gaps as quickly and efficiently as possible

Part of the challenge you face being an agile leader-manager is knowing which hat to wear, when. The technical hat is all about getting the job done, using your technical knowledge and expertise; your leader-manager hat is all about how you get the job done through your team and other resources. An effective leader-manager will constantly be engaging with business issues and considering them from multiple perspectives.

Q. What helps?

A. Three useful beliefs to underpin you as a L-M

Three useful beliefs

Useful belief 1: Exercising authority and accountability

In organisations I work with I see many people who seem to be reluctant to exert authority. Perhaps it's a defence against the old command-and-control culture that used to be prevalent years ago

– or perhaps it's to do with avoiding conflict and upset. If so, the pendulum has swung too far the other way – let's hope we're on our way to equilibrium.

Exerting authority is a necessary element of being an effective leader-manager. Being able to flex and fine tune it is an essential skill. It's often a challenge at first to know just how much authority you can/should bring to bear – and with whom. It takes practice, monitoring and mostly is a case of trial and error. The self-aware, resilient leader-manager is the one who learns from mistakes, bounces back and avoids making the same mistake again.

Engendering accountability in self and others is all about doing what you said you'll do and ensuring others do the same. If others know you take their promises to act seriously, that you'll check progress and action, they are much more likely to deliver. When agreed actions between two or more people are not taken seriously, followed up or discussed, the implicit message is 'it doesn't matter' or 'it's OK to say one thing and do another'.

Good leader-managers hold others accountable for what they say and do. They ask the other person to account for their action – i.e. report back (whether it's done or not, successful or not, started or not finished, etc). They challenge empty excuses such as 'I was too busy'. They let others know they want commitments that will be actioned, not empty platitudes. They challenge impractical timescales or figures, encouraging realism and pragmatism.

Great leader-managers do the same, plus they lead by example and hold themselves accountable – not just to people more senior, but just as importantly, appropriately, to their team members and key stakeholders. They model how it's done in a transparent and businesslike way, offering adjusted timescales and next steps. A great leader-manager is an impressive role model for dependability.

Useful belief 2: Positive effective of working cooperatively

Contrast times when you've worked in a competitive way (doing it your way irrespective of others); a disengaged way (doing the least possible); an accommodating way (doing as you're told); or when you've compromised, sought to find the best of both but without a real sense of 'win-win'.

The difference with working cooperatively and collaboratively is that there is a commitment to a shared goal of win-win; unique result. This is, and can be, a way of working in such a way as to lessen conflict, aggravation, competitiveness and aggression; to mitigate risk; to develop a robust implementation plan that includes not only agreed targets and processes but also makes explicit the exit strategy. This is not something we see commonly – but the advantages are there for the taking; you can use the roadmap to strengthen commitment, drive action, encourage accountability and drive value.

Collaborative business relationships BS11000

In 2014 I became an accredited facilitator of the BS11000 framework. It is the world's first standard for collaborative business relationships. This enables me to help and facilitate organisations to tailor the best of the British Standard BS11000 to their needs. Single companies and partnerships and JVs can gain great value and benefits from the standard; it's in a league of its own because it can be scaled and adapted to meet particular business needs. This means it can be flexibly applied, depending on the context and objectives. Here's a link to the Institute for Collaborative Working http://www.instituteforcollaborativeworking.com/page-1829676

The purpose of collaborative working (using the framework informally or formally) is to promote greater engagement and higher levels of transparency in processes and communications, to improve risk management, to enhance dispute resolution and ultimately to work towards delivering sustainable relationships that deliver value.

In a practical way this enables me to help my clients to

- Facilitate JV leadership teams (separately and together) to build a collaborative working partnership

- Help clients develop their partnering strategies

- Share the message in joint communications

- Facilitate joint workshops, cascading from leadership teams down

- Build joint teams

- Help develop agreed processes, protocols, etc

- Provide independent expertise as and when needed

Useful belief 3: Focus on results and relationships

Keeping the two in mind as you plan, assess progress, work, manage outputs, resolve problems and deal with underperformance leads to a very different approach and is a different experience for all concerned. When the pressure is on to deliver, the focus is usually solely on results; the irony of it is, that when there's pressure to deliver, a focus on conducting interactions with others, demonstrating respect and clear communications in working relationships, can be the difference that makes the difference in delivering the necessary results.

In the heat of the pressure, the busy-ness of multiple tasks and conflicting priorities, it's easy to forget momentarily that it is people who deliver. When relationships are functioning well, when teams are aligned, when people know what they've got to do and have the resources to do it, then results are much more likely to be achieved and targets surpassed.

Ari learned this lesson in his first year as sales manager. He learned that, just because he was a great 'salesman' didn't make him a great leader-manager of the team. He learned to drive results through relationships.

Q. What helps?

A. Play to your strengths and avoid letting your weaknesses define you!

Playing to your strengths works well because you have the personal capacity for the task or action. Even when you're pushed for time you're likely to find it takes less effort, you can execute it easily, efficiently and with more energy. Great leaders, from Churchill to Obama, have appreciated their strengths and the fact that they couldn't do everything themselves or be effective in all areas. They surrounded themselves with others who have different skills, experience or knowledge; people with different strengths from them.

At the same time, everyone has weaknesses. Sometimes they are inherent shortcomings; at other times they could more accurately be described as 'areas for development'. The former are difficult if not impossible to change; the latter are things you can learn, practice and become adept at.

Define weaknesses: (Thesaurus) *'can be to do with powerlessness, frailty, fault and fondness for'*. Words associated with 'weakness' are softness, flawed, faulty, failing, fragility, limitation, at a disadvantage, a drawback, a weak spot, vulnerability, helplessness, predilection, penchant for'.

It can be helpful to think of a weakness as limitation. This means you are (currently) limited by the lack of skill, the fragility of your emotions; you may be at a disadvantage in a certain situation and feel vulnerable. Bear in mind your limitation may be due to lack of willpower or opportunity; it may be a shortcoming in skills or knowledge or it may be low self-confidence and limiting beliefs.

None of these are life-threatening. On the contrary, you can mitigate weaknesses if you're determined to, once you know what they are. For instance, if your confidence is low when preparing for an important interview, you can get help. You can research the internet for good advice, arrange to have coaching to refine skills and practice with feedback; you can reflect back on times when you interviewed well; think of someone you know who's good at interviews and act like them and/or get their advice. What I'm saying here is that you can limit your own actions and achievements if you don't know or don't acknowledge your weaknesses. When you admit them to yourself (and others if necessary) you can do something about them, or at least mitigate against them.

Knowledge is power Awareness is choice

Weaknesses can be a negative; if you can't control your temper there's bound to be fallout with the team or in client meetings. When you deny or refuse to admit your incapability, it can put the project or task in jeopardy. If you're weak at asserting yourself and instead become aggressive or accommodating, there are consequences, some of which will be significant. A leader-manager who is overly accommodating will be recognised as such and people will take advantage. A leader-manager who fails to control aggressive outbursts in fraught situations will fail to build the trust of key stakeholders and may be prone to making impromptu decisions that later do not stand up to scrutiny.

Great L-Ms surround themselves with others
who have complementary and corresponding
skills, knowledge and experience.

Let's face it, some weaknesses or limitations will never be fully overcome – and, pragmatically, some are not worth the time and effort. Your challenge is to distinguish between the ones you can and should overcome or develop – and those that are a wasted effort. In a situation where we feel unable or not as able as others, we feel vulnerable. This is when you need to deploy your strength of character and base your actions on that fact. Remember, every L-M does not need to be as able, as knowledgeable and skilful as everyone around them. Great L-Ms surround themselves with others who have both corresponding and complementary skills, knowledge and experience.

In the world of work, many L-Ms just haven't had the opportunity or the need to develop these 'undeveloped' areas of knowledge or skill. These 'weaknesses' will undermine you if you do nothing to fill the gap. Conversely, if you deal with them by developing the skill or finding someone else with it, you can put your time and efforts into areas where your strengths come to the fore; things get done better and more easily.

> Your 'weaknesses' will undermine unless you
> do something to fill the gap.

The most important thing about shortcomings and areas for development is not to let them define you. You can only do this by being honest with yourself in your self-assessment (no false modesty, no excessive criticism – base it on the facts). It helps to ask for feedback from others who know you in the context, who experience you in the situation and who can give you balanced, objective feedback. If you want feedback, ask for it, be specific … and give them time to think about what they'd like to say.

So, not being defined by your weaknesses requires action. Whenever possible, find others around you (often from your team) who have a complementary skill and get them involved. This requires a level of maturity and an open mind. Some may have the necessary capability there and then; others may need to develop their competence. In the right context, it's in your vested interest, and the interest of the business, for you to develop members of your team. Win-win.

Here are a couple of examples:

Situation 1: Chairing conference calls of your large, geographically-spread project team are difficult for you as you find it almost impossible to distinguish the voices from one another. You prefer face-to-face group meetings, but they're not practical for time and financial reasons.

Opportunity: 'Hi Steph, have you got a sec? I noticed you really enjoyed chairing the conference call on Monday. You did a great job. How you managed all the different threads of conversations was brilliant. Is this something you'd like to get involved with more often?'

Situation 2: Commercial meetings where the client's ops director and the senior geotechnical project manager come along are tricky as your background is in finance, not geotechnical engineering.

Opportunity: One of your geotechnical engineers is showing great promise. He's recently finished a very complex job that has similarities to your client's project. You decide to brief the geo eng thoroughly and invite him along with you for the next meeting. You see this as an opportunity to have support in and after the meeting and he will gain valuable 'client facing' experience.

In essence

- Are you a leader-manager worth following? Just how agile and responsive are you – when things are going well? When things are tough?

- Are you rigorous enough and consistent enough at identifying 'the gap' or do you fall into the trap of jumping to conclusions and action too soon?

- What 'useful belief' above has stretched your levels of awareness?

- To what extent do you know what is needed and expected of you – and are others around you similarly clear?

- Who in your team has natural strengths you could leverage more effectively? Who has shortcomings you've been reluctant to acknowledge?

CHAPTER 8

Conversations for Employee Engagement

Employee engagement and motivation

How much money do you think is saved by employees who are engaged and performing ... in your sector, in your industry, in your country?

What does disengagement cost organisations ... in your sector, in your industry, in your country?

Why is employee engagement important?

Over the past ten years or so employee engagement has become a top business priority for senior executives and I'm sure you're no exception. It's not rocket science to recognise that a highly engaged workforce can increase productivity, innovation and financial performance while reducing costs related to recruitment and retention in highly competitive talent markets.

Employees are the single biggest investment most organisations make, consequently it makes sense to make the most of them and get the best from them. This is not a selfish objective for the business; it's of benefit to the employee too. If you've ever been bored, unmotivated, underutilised or demotivated you will know it becomes uncomfortable and frustrating after a short period of time.

The vast majority of employees want to enjoy their work and make a contribution of some kind to the organisation. While not everyone is wired to be a 'big achiever' it can be easy to undervalue the contribution of those people who come in day after day, week after week, happily doing a good job and getting a sufficient sense of satisfaction from what they do.

Five Conversations for Engagement are central to retaining employees and to maintaining their productivity and loyalty to the organisation. The time and effort required is miniscule in comparison to the cost of failure.

The price of disengagement is huge when you consider significant costs accrue from poor performance and low productivity, absenteeism, employee turnover and the cost of induction and getting someone on board. If we add the cost of lost knowledge, lost skills and the value of loyalty, the figure is staggering. You can calculate the savings made from employee engagement ROI here https://www.officevibe.com/employee-engagement-roi (the figures are in dollars).

Engagement and retention is a major challenge for organisations in many sectors today. The Huffington Post's article in November 2014 reported 13 Disturbing Facts About Employee Engagement, and while this information is US centric, data from UK-based organisations such as CIPD and CIM report similar/equivalent data. http://www.huffingtonpost.com/jeff-fermin/13-disturbing-facts-about_b_6140996.html

> 80% of employees dissatisfied with their direct
> manager are disengaged.
> - Dale Carnegie - Employee Engagement Study

Have you ever estimated how many of your team/employees are 1) motivated, 2) demotivated, 3) unmotivated?

If even 30% of your team fall into the second or third categories, imagine the consequences. Imagine too, if you were able to re-engage, remotivate, recapture their commitment, what a difference to productivity and the wider environment it would make.

Also consider the costs of the demotivated and unmotivated employees on their colleagues and peers. Demotivation in particular is like a virus. It can be catching – and the impact can be fast and lasting ... whinging, complaining, lateness, increased absences, mistakes and errors, late submissions, inaccuracies, low-quality work, rumours, negativity, speculation, to mention just a few.

Harvard Business Review reports regularly and robustly on all things 'leadership and management', and the following are stats from late 2013. Just as with results from Gallup over the past 25 years, similar drivers crop up year after year after year. No rocket science here either.

What employees want are recognition, engagement, clarity and opportunity. Simple.

Most Impactful Employee Engagement Drivers

How important are each of the following in terms of
their impact on employee engagement?

Top box scores for all respondents (8-10)

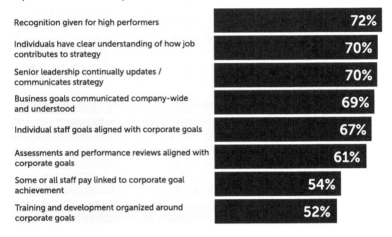

Recognition given for high performers	72%
Individuals have clear understanding of how job contributes to strategy	70%
Senior leadership continually updates / communicates strategy	70%
Business goals communicated company-wide and understood	69%
Individual staff goals aligned with corporate goals	67%
Assessments and performance reviews aligned with corporate goals	61%
Some or all staff pay linked to corporate goal achievement	54%
Training and development organized around corporate goals	52%

https://hbr.org/resources/pdfs/comm/achievers/hbr_achievers_report_
sep13.pdf

Fig. 31 Most Impactful Employee Engagement Drivers (stats)

A word about motivation

I'm not going to deal with motivation as a subject matter in this book
as there's so much already available on the subject. However, I will
add a few thoughts in the context of engagement and developing
and maintaining relationships that engender productivity and
success.

Motivation and engagement are part of the same equation.
Motivation is all around drive and values. For instance, if financial
security is important to you, then having and keeping a job that
provides the salary package in the kind of organisation you can
perform well in will be high on your values list. If having recognition
and acknowledgment from your boss or colleagues motivates you,
then having that will be high on your value list.

Amazing relationships deliver amazing results.

One of the key responsibilities for any leader-manager is to motivate, engage and retain their employees. The job of leader-managers is not only about task completion and results; while they are an important ultimate outcome, your priorities are to focus on how those tasks and results get delivered and the people who deliver them. This means doing whatever you can (and if you can't, getting help from others) to build and invest regularly in your relationships with team members.

There is no substitute for personal connection. If you can build a 'personal bank account' with others and keep in credit, you will be able to draw on it in tough times, without paying the highest price.

There's no substitute for talking to people face to face (or by phone when that is not possible). 'Amazing relationships deliver amazing results' is a useful motto for any leader-manager with responsibility for people.

Conversations for:

The good news is you know that it is a fact that employees want recognition, engagement, clarity and opportunity. Everything in this book will serve you in helping your team and your direct reports to be as productive and engaged as possible. Furthermore, when you take the approaches included here and apply your understanding to the different conversations that are often needed, you can improve your skills and success as a leader-manager – and your own sense of success and fulfilment.

Retention

You are a busy person. Manage your team and resources well by ensuring that every conversation you conduct has a purpose. Over weeks and months as you do your job you'll find yourself having a multitude of conversations. Some of them are random and relatively purposeless, such as catching up with friends and colleagues, chatting over coffee or in the lift.

You'll also have more formal conversations in one-to-one and group situations. These are more likely to have some purpose, such as progress review, updating, reporting back, planning meetings, negotiations, selection interviews, appraisal reviews ... and many more.

Undoubtedly, major issues around fair treatment, competence, conditions, opportunities and problems may well cause 'engagement' problems with employees. These need to be addressed – but so do the smaller things that bother and annoy your employees. The challenge with some of these is that they can seem trivial to you or others, but not to the individual who is being affected by them.

Story: Helen is a customer services adviser for a high-end retailer and has been in her role for over nine months. She enjoys the role and gets on extremely well with her manager and colleagues in the busy office in central London. At least that was true until one day relatively soon after her manager left the organisation, and a new manager was appointed. Within days, team members came into work to find the seating arrangements had changed without discussion. She now found herself seated with five other colleagues, all of whom were 5-10 years older than her and all very big personalities and very chatty. Helen found it difficult to concentrate and she felt intimidated by some of them. She spoke to the new manager who didn't see this as an issue. She told Helen, 'You'll get used to it. Just give them as good as you get.' Three weeks on, Helen says she feels stressed most days as she finds it difficult to focus on her customers. She is still performing but her engagement is slipping. It's likely she's a retention risk.

How would you handle a quiet member of staff who came to you like this?

How would you handle a conversation with someone you knew to be a retention risk?

What are the costs of inaction?

How would you handle the wider issues this scenario raises?

Clarity

'The greatest challenge with communication
is the illusion that it has taken place.'
-Oscar Wilde

A manager I used to work for had a favourite challenge; she used to say, *Just because it's clear in my head and I tell you, doesn't mean you understand it in the same way – so let's always double check we understand the same thing'*. What a wise woman she was; she knew from her own and others' experience that the outgoing message is always filtered by the incoming receiver. Those filters alter the nature of what is heard and understood, and comparing the messages offers an opportunity to clarify, correct, re-emphasise, explain, etc.

Roles and responsibilities:

A frequent area with a need for 'clarity' is roles and responsibilities at work. When you think about it, the workplace is a much more dynamic, complicated and unpredictable place these days. Fewer people doing more with less means individual team members and colleagues often have a greater workload.

Virtual and geographically spread teams and team members work part-time or job-share and have overlapping responsibilities for tasks and projects. This may result in team members doing the task they most prefer or one they're good at or enjoy and not doing those they dislike or are not as competent at.

As organisations are flatter now, there's lots of opportunity for things to fall through the cracks, unless the team is aligned and on the same page regarding tasks.

Don't be surprised that when these overlaps in responsibilities happen, you have greater responsibility to conduct a series of conversations in order to achieve clarity about responsibilities, standards and obligations.

Promises/Broken Promises

Another reason for conversations for clarity springs from promises made. If you promise a promotion or opportunity to someone, make sure it happens. If for some reason it won't or can't, then prepare well for what may be a serious disappointment before you tell the person.

One of the most dispiriting stories I have heard was of a middle manager who had been promised promotion to the next level when the team expanded and a new role was created.

> **Story:** PJ had terrific technical skills, was well liked and respected in the team, dependable and motivated to progress. Out of the blue (as far as he was concerned) a new recruit joined the department and within three months was promoted into the role PJ had been promised. Needless to say, PJ's line manager had to face up to having a 'courageous conversation' with PJ. In the event, the conversation was poorly handled. In a period of a few months the department went from having a highly engaged, motivated and technically effective member of staff in PJ, to one who felt mistreated and demotivated and now harboured a lack of trust. I'm not saying the decision to recruit an external person into role was a poor one; how it was handled is the issue here.

Realignment of performance

Loss of Focus

Everyone becomes preoccupied from time to time, with issues at work or in private lives. These can range, for instance, from health or relationships to financial troubles, and they can show up at work in the quality, speed of work, lack of focus on priorities, difficulty concentrating, responsiveness to requests, etc. When the situation reaches a certain level of seriousness that is difficult to deal with, focus shifts to that area of concern and away from others 'less pressing' (in that context).

In this situation, a conversation with the person about how best to recover the necessary level of performance is required; to explore what will help and to manage both parties' expectations about what is acceptable and what isn't. Where their health is concerned, it will make sense to involve occupational health. Having the conversation can illuminate not just the symptoms and causes, but also the way forward – and awareness by all the relevant people means support can be given and action taken.

Customer complaint (need to learn new skills)

The sales arena is a demanding one. I know this from my experience working with Toyota, Ford and Lexus. Weekly, monthly, quarterly and annual targets are set and measurement is unrelenting. In the best motor trade companies they exercise precision in target setting such as I have never experienced before. It's really admirable. While the focus is on selling vehicles and associated products, an enormous focus for sales executives is on customer satisfaction. It's not only about what they are selling but how the customer perceived the experience. Customer satisfaction is consistently measured and often incentivised. What the customer thinks and feels really counts and when a customer complains, it is taken very seriously.

Story: Dave and the new car customer. A new customer came into the salesroom on Saturday afternoon. He was accompanied by his wife and they had never bought a brand new car before. He told the sales executive that he'd seen the sales deals online and that he had done his research online. He assured the sales exec that he knew exactly what he wanted and how much he would pay. It was clear that the customer had massive expectations and apparent confidence – and this meant he presented with what could be described as a bullish attitude to getting what he wanted.

As the discussion progressed, he asked for a number of 'add-ons' that were not part of the marketed sales deal. The sales exec calmly explained what options were available, but the customer was not listening. Perhaps he was grandstanding in front of his wife and he said he was not prepared to negotiate.

Eventually, the conversation escalated and the customer's temper flared when told by the sales exec that the deal he wanted was not possible. There was no profit in that deal for the dealership. The customer complained to the general manager. In the event, the sales exec was correct in terms of procedure; however, a conversation was necessary with the sales exec in terms of his inability to handle conflict and rudeness from the customer, so that in future he would be more competent at handling complaints and maintaining his composure under pressure.

Change to Team Structure (realignment of performance)

Organisations need to change and adapt in order to be both proactive and responsive to commercial realities, financial competition, sector expansion and technical growth. When these changes occur it will be apparent immediately in some cases that a change in team structure is necessary. In other cases, it can take time before the need to change the team structure become evident. When this happens, conversations about redeployment, relocation, revised role requirements, refocused responsibilities, redundancy and promotion come into play and you as a manager are required to have the conversation.

The easy bit is speaking to those who want to stay and for whom there is a role they are happy about (redeployment, promotion, refocused role). The more difficult bit is when it comes to redundancy, relocation and revised role requirements, especially when there is resistance within the team to changing their routines, working hours/ habits and the processes they are firmly attached to.

Story: Ian is head of HR in a geographically spread retail service company, functioning across the UK and Ireland. The organisation had grown over the past ten years and while the latest recession slowed sales and decreased attrition, now things were picking up. Investment in infrastructure and expansion in locations meant the need for a more robust and less labour-intensive HR system. This required the administrators to change how they processed information (computerising everything, sharing data, multitasking within HR rather than everyone being a specialist in one area). The other change required was to shift from being a totally responsive service to one of taking a more proactive 'service' approach so as to involve and enable line managers out in the business to access and utilise the new system. Ian's challenge was to prepare for, assess and then conduct conversations with team members in both locations, to establish their confidence, competence and willingness to change.

As part of his preparation, Ian clearly identified the new role competencies and experience required and he had written new role profiles/job descriptions. He was clear going into the conversations where areas of negotiation existed and where they didn't. This helped him stay focused and consistent in his message when the going got tough.

Challenge

Challenge can be both positive and constructive. The purpose of challenging conversations is to change, improve or enhance current performance. These can be the encouraging, inspiring, reassuring, persuading, uplifting kind of challenge; or the challenge that is judgmental or critical. You're more likely to get a better response from the former.

1. Challenge to change their behaviour Managers often report that one of the trickiest situations to deal with is when a direct report (and occasionally a line manager or client) has an aggressive or belligerent attitude. Aggressive behaviour so often begets aggressive behaviour. A pattern of behaviour sets in and it is difficult to break the pattern because it becomes a vicious circle. Breaking the pattern is possible, at least temporarily. As with so many behaviours, getting to the root cause of the behaviour will help you understand whether the best you can hope for is a 'temporary ceasefire' or whether sustained change is possible.

2. Challenge to stretch them: making the tasks and objectives tougher; stretching them to achieve more with the same resources, faster and of higher quality; encouraging a different approach that takes them out of their comfort zone; inspiring them to take a calculated risk; stimulating their intellect to problem solve more effectively.

3. Challenge to change their attitude via constructive feedback: for jumping to conclusions without any reflection; sloppy inaccurate work; repeated lateness/absence; uncooperative, sullen, aggressive behaviour; cynicism that discourages others; failure to do what they said they would – again.

These are all conversations a L-M needs to have. Some L-Ms are good at all, others are uncomfortable at one, two or all three? That's where the skill-will gap exists. Is this 'gap' for you? Something you'd like to be more effective at and feel comfortable doing?

How would you deal with Barry?

Barry, a senior manager, was considered in the company to be quite brilliant technically but it was felt his people skills left a lot to be desired. His new line manager's first conversation with Barry was a shocker. In a one-to-one call the L-M asked Barry to give him an overview of the project and a description of what the issues were. Barry said in a gruff tone, 'I don't have time for this b******t. *Find out from someone else,' and put the phone down. When they met later that week, Barry apologised and said it was because he was under stress to finish a client report. Over the following weeks, the new L-M saw rude and aggressive behaviour a number of times in Barry's interactions at work. A conversation for challenge was diarised.*

Disappointment

Whenever you have to tell people something that will disappoint them, you can reasonably expect an emotional reaction. Disappointment implies a refusal, setback or failure and with it comes some level of regret, frustration, disillusionment, disenchantment or even distress. Denial, too, can be a response, as it's a protective reaction in response to disappointment.

In the work context, these are a few common reasons you will come across. Some reflect your disappointment with them, their performance, attitude, behaviour, etc. Others relate to their disappointment with circumstances and opportunities.

Which of these conversations for disappointment can you relate to?

- they haven't been successful in their application for a job/ or promotion

- a stronger candidate for a role or task is available

- you haven't been able to deliver the promised promotion/ opportunity

- they failed to deliver on their promised level of performance
- they are just not competent for the task/project, despite their willingness and motivation
- they arrived unprepared for a meeting, despite your support
- they failed to stand up for their idea and present compelling evidence in the face of strong opposition
- their performance is hit and miss, inconsistent at a time when results matter
- they failed to have an essential 'difficult conversation' with one of the team
- they are utilising their authority in an inappropriate manner
- they exercised poor decision making
- they failed to deliver results needed, on time
- they lost their temper in a team meeting
- they were insensitive/hurtful to another member of the team experiencing difficulties
- they bottled giving bad news to a client – and left it to someone else
- they failed to hold one of the team accountable for their actions and consequences were severe

Story: Darren was one of the most positive managers in the business and a good performer. He worked hard, came into work early and frequently left late. His pleasing nature was both his strength and his weakness. It was a massive strength when dealing with customers, many of whom returned again and again because of him. However, his drive to please others became a weakness when his accommodating nature meant he did not push sales and profit levels as hard as was needed for him to achieve his targets.

Recent results were hit and miss and his line manager wanted more consistency from Darren. As she watched him one day she knew he was overempathising with his customers who, he knew, didn't want to 'overpay' for the service.

She was aware that Darren was confident and competent – yet he wasn't delivering to his potential. She sat down with him and expressed her disappointment in recent results and worked with him, taking a coaching approach to refocus his performance in such a way that he maximised his strengths without going into empathy overdrive.

In essence

- Your impact as a leader-manager in retaining and engaging others is greater than you probably imagine.

- You have massive power every single day – and massive responsibility to engage employees, on behalf of the business.

- Engagement and retention is a major challenge for organisations today and the influence of leader-managers in retaining performing employees is critical.

- Research on employee engagement over years consistently reports that recognition, engagement, role clarity and opportunity are key drivers.

- One-to-one conversations are at the heart of relationships and an investment in a five-minute conversation can save you time and effort and prevent breakdown in performance and team relationships.

- Proactivity in having conversations for challenge, clarity, disappointment, retention, etc, are at the heart of effectiveness of your role as leader-manager. Gather your courage. Do your preparation. Focus on what's necessary.

- Bring backbone and heart into each purposeful conversation in order to salvage retrievable situations before the situation becomes acute and the behaviours entrenched.

CHAPTER 9

Handling Difficult 'Courageous' Conversations

Conversation for impact and buy-in

In this chapter we will explore the following:

Why? The importance of facing up to and conducting difficult conversations.

What? A range of conversations – how each is similar yet different.

How? How to prepare for the conversation, or a series of conversations.

How to effect the necessary changes using a guided pathway to help you have constructive dialogue that gets a beneficial result – using steps you can move up, down and through.

Introduction

How many times have you sat in your office inwardly groaning at the thought of the conversation you know you must have? Perhaps it's an item on your 'to do' list such as 'speak to Chris' or 'tell Alex the bad news' or 'lay the law down with John', and if you're honest, it's been on the list for too long. One way or another it is something you know you need to face up to; get it over and done with. *Carpe diem*. Perhaps the fact that you're reading this is a sign that now is the right time.

When you ask yourself why you haven't done it yet, your reasons will stretch from 'I haven't found the right opportunity'; 'I've been snowed under'; 'They've been on leave' and 'It's so awkward' to 'They'll blow their top' and many more (some of which may well be excuses (see previous chapter). In this chapter we'll explore these reasons and come up with some strategies you can use to move forward, one way or another.

Time, opportunity, busy-ness, conflicting schedules are most commonly presented first. If you dig down, reasons include previous efforts were not successful and the wish to avoid conflict. Anticipation of confrontation, lack of know-how and confidence dealing with/resolving conflict, poor communication between the parties, lack of patience and frustration all appear as causes.

When the meeting finally takes place, both parties find that one of the reasons these conversations are difficult is that they evolve into 'monologues' rather than being dialogues. The manager often launches into the problem, the situation, the issues, the blame, without any preamble.

What's common in 'difficult conversations' is the difference between what makes the conversation easy and what makes it difficult. I frequently ask managers I work with, 'What would make this an easy/easier conversation to hold?' It's astonishing how often the answer is something like 'I just need to stop and think what I'd say' or 'I need to make the time'.

Fig. 32 Bridging the gap

What would bridge the gap ... make this an
easy/easier conversation to hold?

Consequently, not only is it possible but usually it's quite 'solvable' if they put their mind to it. Granted, it may take some planning; it may not take place right away today, but more often than not, they can make it happen within a short space of time.

Any resistance to having the conversation that crops up later needs dealing with in a similar manner. As you now know from having read that chapter of the book, each 'objection' (as some of my sales managers would put it) needs to be dealt with, one at a time.

What most often gets obscured in the haze of emotion and feelings of anxiety that surround handling difficult conversations is the true purpose of the conversation. This can range from problem performance, dependability, quality of output, timekeeping, workload management, lack of focus on priorities, promised action not taken, belligerent attitude, absence of cooperation with others, repeated errors, lack of dependability, negative (whinging) attitude, disengagement with the team and many more.

That's why this chapter is such an important one in the arsenal of any leader-manager and why we'll be exploring the why, what and how of **necessary, difficult conversations**.

Why handle difficult conversations?

Have you ever asked yourself 'Who'd notice if I didn't have that (difficult) conversation?' You may be tempted at first to think the answer is 'no one', but you and I both know the honest answer is – plenty of people.

When there's a performance issue with someone in the team, project or department, the truth is that most people know about the clash of personalities, poor attitude, sloppy work, aggressive attitude, underperformance, the demotivation, the disloyalty, etc.

Individuals may not be fixated about it; they may not worry about it constantly; they may not even complain or comment about it unless they're asked, but don't ever kid yourself that they don't know. They know about the issue and they know what you, as line manager, as leader-manager, are doing or are not doing about it. There are few secrets when it comes to issues that trouble the team.

> Constructive dialogue is about getting
> results and maintaining a good
> working relationship.

The truth is, employees look to their leader-manager for support in dealing with and resolving the challenges that arise at work. Not only that, it is the responsibility of a L-M to deal with issues in the team or department. That is your job. Avoiding it is not the answer. The stakes may be high at the time of the conversation, but the real cost kicks in when they are avoided and the issues fester or escalate.

The power of how you think

There's much discussion and greater appreciation nowadays as to the extent to which our thinking drives our behaviour. 'If you think you can or you think you can't you're probably right.' Consequently, before we go into 'how' to have these conversations, I want to acknowledge how our thinking affects us as we think about the situation/person; not just whether we 'step up and have the conversation' but 'how' we conduct them when we do.

One of the most impactful books I've read in the last ten year is *Loving What Is* by Byron Katie. Her proposition in the book is a simple fact that (in the words of the Greek philosopher Epictetus):

'We are disturbed not by what happens to us, but by our thoughts about what happens'.

By using Katie's process of inquiry, we 'discover that all the concepts and judgments that we believe or take for granted are distortions of things as they really are. When we believe our thoughts instead of what is really true for us, we experience all kinds of suffering'.

So often, when we conduct difficult conversations, the outcome for us and/or others is a kind of suffering. This is the key reason why leader-managers – and most of the rest of the population – resist facing up to them. If all leader-managers read her book, their thinking would certainly be different … and difficult conversations would be a very different and less stressful experience. I commend the book to you.

The principle of the 'self-fulfilling prophecy' works in a similar way … and has consequences:

- If you believe a meeting is going to go badly… it often does

- If you believe that someone won't be cooperative… they often aren't

- If you believe people will be helpful … they often are

- If you believe they will understand where you're coming from … they often will

- … and whether they do or not, you have to deal with it.

In general, I find leader-managers quick to action, decision making and problem solving. Some I work with just love jumping straight into a challenge without giving it much thought at all. Engineers frequently tell me, 'It's my job to solve problems and get the job done.' They're right. BUT, this doesn't mean acting without thinking.

'How well (or not) does how you think about handling difficult conversations serve you?'

'What would change if you took a more confident approach?'

The speed may be necessary, but more often it's born of habit. The pressure to 'do something' (jump to action and solutions) is so strong in most organisations and with little explicit encouragement to 'stop and think before you act', it's no wonder mistakes, wrong conclusions, accidents and re-work are so commonplace. 'Speak now, think later' is the order of the day; how different the culture of the organisation would be if everyone were actively encouraged to 'stop and think, before you speak or act'.

By the way, any despair I feel comes not from a place of criticism, but from a place of knowing that even 10 to 15 minutes' focused preparation can make a significant difference – especially in circumstances where emotions are heated.

What would you do if you weren't afraid?

Think back to that 'difficult conversation' on your to-do list that I mentioned at the beginning of the chapter. What if you didn't go into 'catastrophic thinking' mode; avoided all your gremlin reasons for not having the conversation? What if you didn't *think* of the conversation as 'difficult'? What if, instead, you began to think of them as 'courageous conversations'; interactions and discussions that need you, as a leader-manager (and often as a line manager) to find your courage, step up to the inherent challenge and execute as effectively as you can.

What's needed for handling difficult situations successfully?

In an earlier chapter we looked at the need to think and plan before you act. Those principles have just as much relevance in the context of conducting constructive dialogues or difficult conversations.

1. **Awareness and ability** to identify there is an issue and the self-awareness and confidence to cope with it effectively (if not, the willingness to get help with the 'how')

2. **Preparation for and practice** having the constructive dialogue; and ability to discuss and agree a way forward (see next section)

3. **Act** to effect the necessary change, i.e. get the right result

4. **Review it to reinforce or tweak ...** to make it stick.

You'll read much more about these later in this chapter.

A Guided Pathway: A process for constructive Courageous Conversations: before, during and after

The need to conduct difficult conversations is evident from all you've been reading so far. The question of 'how' is now what needs to be tackled. How do you conduct a difficult conversation in such a way that it gives you both a good chance of coming out of it in a better state then you went in. You'll notice, more often than not, I refer to these as 'courageous conversations', rather than difficult conversations.

The reason for this is simple and comes from my personal experience and viewpoint. If I'm anticipating or in the middle of a 'difficult conversation' and I'm thinking about it as 'difficult', it reinforces how difficult it is. Instead, over the past few years I've come to think about them as 'courageous conversations'; because of the challenge they hold, I need to find courage to face up to and conduct them – and the courage to see them through.

Uses for the Guided Pathway for Courageous Conversations

The following 3-stage, 7-step process gives you a pathway that can be helpful in a wide range of 'difficult conversations' including:

- a worrying change in behaviour that's affecting their/others' performance

- checking out underlying reasons for changing their mind on a decision

- exploring their understanding of the gap in performance/ behaviour

- giving constructive feedback on a disappointment/failure to achieve standards/their loss of focus

- challenging/encouraging someone to step up and take massive/proactive/corrective action

- conducting an informal underperformance discussion

- asking for a promotion/career break

- dealing with poor service delivery/mistake by a contractor

- asserting yourself with a client about a difference of opinion

- clarifying a misunderstanding

- discussing a difference of opinion

- asking your boss about a delayed promotion/increase in salary

- talking to your child about poor exam results

- … and many others

The anticipation of the conversation is sometimes worse than the conversation itself. Tension and worry that it won't go well and 'I'll make it worse not better' raise stress levels. The possibility exists that, because the parties involved may have different perspectives (or agendas) or may think they do, the conversations could well go off course.

> 'I need to find courage to face up to and conduct them – and then courage to follow through.' – Mike, Sales Exec, Retail

Managers have reported this happening numerous times – it's only after the conversation is over that they realise they 'never quite got to the point' and no satisfactory resolution was achieved. When you're stressed, you don't think straight; if there are two in the conversation, little value can come from no one thinking straight.

Start with the end in mind: Use the 3-Stage, 7-Step Process

In order to give you a better-than-evens chance that you'll not only conduct an effective conversation, it will be useful to have a structure that helps you stay on track. The process I'll show you below started when we were developing a new workshop for a client. Over the past few years I have revised, refined and added to it. It's now called 3-7, which stands for a **3-stage, 7-step** process for handling courageous conversations. It's based on Deming's PDCA process and I'm proud to say it's being used by hundreds of managers across the UK and Ireland.

3-7

3-7 offers structure in preparing for, executing and following up any 'courageous conversation' – 3 = before, during and after. These easy-to-remember stages represent the '3' and using them brings you greater precision, rigour and progression.

Once you're in the middle of the difficult conversation, it can be easy to get drawn into other matters. As a L-M, it's your job to notice the conversation has gone off at a tangent and to get the conversation back on track. If and when it happens (and it surely will), you can acknowledge the tangent and then bring the conversation back on track.

> *'Mike, I notice we've veered away from what we came to discuss, namely why you didn't submit that report on time – and we've moved to talking about an issue with the IT system. You're right, the IT issue needs to be sorted out, so let's explore that in this afternoon's meeting. Right now, let's get back to discussing your late report to the client that's caused so much trouble.'*

When you take control of the conversation, you demonstrate both leadership and management in action. You're showing both reasonableness and laser-like focus on the issue at hand. Use 3-7 and it will help you regain the control and direction of the meeting, so as to achieve the intended aim.

> 'Staff quickly learn whether you can be distracted or not – and if you can be, especially in a difficult conversation about them, they'll use it to their advantage.'
> – Mike M, Project Manager, Construction

The courageous conversation itself is formed of 7 steps, structured to encourage and enable both parties to contribute and to move from problem to solution. Some issues may require more than one conversation, which may be to do with complexity of the issue, quality of the relationships, the need for further investigation, etc. Like any set of steps, it allows you to go back and forth as needed to progress.

Some 'courageous conversations' go smoothly and roughly follow the pathway. In others, it feels as though it's 'two steps forward, one step back' at times during the conversation. Think of the

7 steps as being like a piece of orchestral music. Each musician learns their part thoroughly, so that when it's their turn to play, it is well timed and accurate. Precision is the first goal. Once that is achieved, the conductor may encourage members to improvise. The best improvisations come 'after' the musicians have thoroughly familiarised themselves with the music as it was written by the composer.

As you know, practice makes perfect; getting the 7 steps 'in the muscle', as we've discussed earlier in the book, will stand you in terrific stead when it comes to facing, handling and staying in control of awkward discussions. Use the 7 steps multiple times; review what you did well, what worked, what you need to tweak each time.

Practice five or six times in a short period of time, making improvements each time. You will notice your skills and confidence grow. Don't worry if you make the occasional blip; it happens. Review what happened and plan how not to repeat it. Put it behind you and move on.

If you find yourself thinking there aren't the opportunities to practice at work – use the 7 steps at home or in other aspects of your life.

> 'I decided I would be like a dog with a bone in practicing the 7 steps. The first few times weren't brilliant; but I used it over and over and eventually got the hang of it. Now I'm much more confident and the 3-7 is working well.' – Sarah, HR Manager

The important thing to remember is that when you use this pathway, it can help you identify where you are in the conversation, help you get back on track and move towards a constructive ending.

3-7: The Courageous Conversation Pathway:

Stage 1: Prepare well before the conversation

Never approach a difficult, unpredictable, uncertain conversation without doing your prep. The same rule applies for any situation where you are looking to exert influence and persuasion, where you care about the outcome and want to set yourself and the other person up for success.

Prepare the case. While 15 minutes good thinking space will help, I highly recommend you spend more like 30 minutes or more on your preparation; it will pay dividends.

- Understand the 'real' situation

- Collect the facts; what evidence do you have? What's the gap?

- Gain perspective on the context. What is the reality?

- Hear from others who have valid input

- Get data, stats

- Go and see with your own eyes (the evidence, the place, the person, etc)

- Find out what actions were taken (and why, if appropriate to context)

- Consider what outcomes you want (or the business wants) from this conversation

- Examine resistors (yours and the other person's)

- Anticipate objections, excuses, reasons, etc

In other words, be as fully prepared as you can be, with facts, rather than assumptions or opinions.

> Find your courage, step up to the inherent
> challenge and execute the discussion as
> effectively as you can. Then review.

As part of your preparation, consider the following:

Who you are dealing with? How do they respond under pressure (as they will likely feel under pressure in this conversation)? What can you do to build rapport with them at the beginning, to reduce tension? What can you say that reassures them you wish to get to the truth of the matter and resolve it in a constructive way? What winds them up, so you can avoid doing it? How will you avoid 'losing it' if the conversation gets heated? How can you put across the facts, evidence, your perspective in a way they understand?

How you will build rapport? Because these conversations by their very nature feel difficult, awkward or risky, defensiveness is never far away. Therefore, at the start of the conversation (and at any time necessary during the meeting) use approaches, questions, etc, to build rapport with the person, as appropriate to the context. The aim is to lower defences (yours and theirs) and to enable a calm, logical conversation that results in clarity on the situation, resolution of the issue or some movement forward together.

Collect evidence/facts In some conversations, such as performance management conversations about attitude, hard evidence may be harder to find; some of it may be 'perception' as opposed to facts. All the more reason to be cautious – and courageous – as the conversation still needs to be conducted. If it's about their changed attitude, gather examples that are as specific as possible, so that you can use them effectively. And avoid saying their attitude has changed for the worse and not be able to back this up credibly.

> Conducting courageous conversations can bring out the best or the worst in us. You choose which you want it to be.

Get back on track These conversations can go off track when other issues are raised, when someone else is blamed for the issue, when other unresolved or festering issues are introduced into the conversation as a defence or distraction, etc. If you recognise this is happening, acknowledge the issue and 'park' it, to be discussed at another time, then use this 7-step pathway to help you identify where you are in the conversation, help you get back on track and move towards a constructive ending.

Stage 2: Conducting the conversation

Note: *The order given below is important* and I suggest you follow the order closely while you learn the steps. Once you have it 'in the muscle' you may find you go back and forth with some steps, delving deeper into the situation or the solutions.

Step 1: Put the person at their ease and explain why you're speaking to them. Show respect by speaking to them privately (not in front of others). Tell them what you want to talk to them about. The atmosphere may range from informal to encouraging and exploratory, through more formal to disciplinary.

Step 2: Get their views – ask for their perspective on the issue – 'how they see it'. As they speak, listen, note down key words/phrases to help you remember. Listen, don't interrupt while they speak.

Repeat what you've understood and clarify any necessary details.

Step 3: Give your views – calmly describe 'how you see it'. This leaves room for open dialogue about the differences in opinion. You share your understanding of the situation, giving specific examples of behaviour/attitude you have found evidence of so there's no misunderstanding. **Base the dialogue on fact, not opinions.**

It's common to loop backwards and forwards through steps 1 – 3 while the issues are being discussed and views shared. If rapport is lost and emotions heighten, either regain rapport or take a short comfort break before continuing the discussion. In some circumstances, it may be helpful to reconvene later.

Step 4: The turnaround. Finding common ground – find some aspect of the solution you have in common. For example, you both want to find a resolution; to avoid untimely delays; to save time/money; to find a way forward both of you can live with, etc.

Step 5: Resolve differences – encourage them to suggest ideas about how it can be resolved. Get their buy-in by asking 'how can this be resolved?'; 'how else?'; 'what else?'; 'who else?' Add your own ideas after they've contributed.

Step 6: Agree action and accountability – aim for specific actions, SMART (see below). First ask for suggestions, offer options, then discuss; offer practical assistance; agree they will flag any delays or difficulties with you, and how.

Summarise SMART actions for yourself and them; agree clearly how they are accountable to you (or others) for their actions; notify when the review will take place.

Setting SMART Objectives

This is a systematic way to set goals, targets and objectives and enables you to do so in a clear and understandable way. There's lots on the internet about writing and agreeing SMART objectives but for now here's what it stands for:

Specific

Measurable

Achievable

Relevant and realistic

Time framed

Stage 3: Step 7 After the conversation

Step 7: Review and consolidate – Having put a date/time in the diary to check and monitor progress, support/challenge/enable as necessary. Review as agreed. Dismiss, continue or escalate, as appropriate.

Warning: It's important to COMPLETE this stage/step. It's easy to skip either because the issue has been resolved, or because it hasn't been. Be thorough. Close the circle.

> When the 'courageous conversation' issue is resolved, your joint success deserves to be acknowledged.

It will have taken effort and action to achieve success and this deserves recognition. Whether or not resolution is achieved, this stage/step is important. Your reputation as a L-M is never more on the line than in challenging circumstances.

If the issue is not resolved or remains incomplete, a further review to acknowledge progress and plan for further action is necessary. Without this, the effects of earlier efforts may be lost. Failure by the L-M to follow through also sends a powerful message and may be interpreted in a number of ways, not all helpful. Indeed the L-M's reputation may be affected.

CHECKLIST for your 3-7: Courageous Conversation

Before The Conversation: Prepare

- ❑ Get your facts straight, Get your facts straight
- ❑ Collect evidence, examples, details. Identify gaps in knowledge, evidence
- ❑ Prepare your approach
- ❑ Consider what outcome you are looking for (for you/them/the business)
- ❑ Ask them to prepare for the meeting. Ask them to think about the context – motivation, performance, attitude, responsibilities, skill gap, etc …
- ❑ … or in the context of poor performance discussion eg timekeeping, absence, attitude, task completion, etc

During The Conversation

Follow the 7-step pathway; it gives you a path to follow and allows you to go with the flow of the conversation while staying on the path, eventually coming to some kind of resolution or way forward.

1. **Put them at their ease** and tell them why you're speaking to them

2. **Get their views** – and listen. Repeat what you've understood and clarify

3. **Give your views**. Use facts not opinions

4. **Turnaround.** Find common ground (shared benefits) for mutual resolution; link to what they value

5. Resolve differences **to gain buy-in**. Ask, 'How can this be resolved?'; 'How else?'; 'What else?'

6. **Agree specific action.** Ask for suggestions. Summarise SMART actions for yourself and them

7. Set a date/time to **review.** Diarise it. Check progress

After The Conversation

Having put date/time in diary

- Monitor progress/lack of progress

- Reinforce positive progress

- Discuss progress – informally or formally

- Support/challenge/assert/enable

- Praise and acknowledge progress; close out; continue; escalate … as appropriate.

Fig. 33 Checklist for 3-7 Conversation

Overcoming the barriers to holding Courageous Conversations

Remember, as I said before, what we're exploring here is the why, what and how of *necessary conversations*.

Now that we've explored the reasons why conducting constructive dialogues are vital and you have a structured process to follow … what else could get in the way?

I asked myself this recently when I noticed I was prevaricating about a necessary courageous conversation. I dithered for days then I examined my 'why'. Scribbling my thoughts on paper, I used this simple format to help me find a way to action.

The following are phrases managers frequently mention. I've added stratagems to help you get from avoidance to action. Good luck.

Avoidance phrases	Stratagems to get me into action
"My diary is stacked"	If it needs to be done, make time. Allow 10-15 minutes to prep and 15-20 minutes for the conversation. If you're a manager and can't find 30 minutes to do your job… You shouldn't be a manager.
Location – "It's too far to go"	Arrange travel; if not practical, live with the fact. Organise a video conference, use Facetime or Skype so that you have eye contact. If not, telephone works too.
"They're a friend"	Then be a friend. Tell them the truth. Acknowledge it's difficult – and do it. Trust yourself. Trust them.
"I'll do it next time I see them"	If it's urgent it's time to face the fear and do it anyway. If it's important and not urgent, do it this week. Send an Outlook invitation.
"Not enough time today/this week"	if it is important, make time in the next 5 working day. If it's urgent find 15-20 minutes for the conversation today or tomorrow. No excuses.
"It'll sort itself out"	Chances are, it won't. It's much more likely to recur. Do the right thing; have the conversation; protect your reputation.

"Last time went badly"	Find the gutsy part of you. Allow for why it went badly. Be gentle with yourself; it's a learning curve. Build your confidence by taking steps to recover it.
"I don't want to upset them"	Use this empathy rather than have it exploit you. Remember, it may be necessary for them to be upset before they'll change.
"Maybe I've got the wrong end of the stick"	Gather your evidence and act on it. Speak to others you trust. Establish if / where there's a gap in evidence. Operate on this principle in the discussion.
"I'm sure it won't happen again"	Chances are it may. If it does, what are you (through your inaction) colluding with? Do the right thing; have the conversation. Help them get back on course.
"It could make things worse"	It's true; it is a risk. It could get worse. It could get worse before it gets better. Trust that you have the skills to deal with it and the obligation on behalf of the business, do the right thing.

Fig. 34 Dealing with avoidance phrases

Twenty things to BE when handling Courageous Conversations

These conversations can bring out the best or the worst in us. You choose which you want it to be. In the face of a range of people with whom you interact, here are 20 suggestions of how you can choose to 'be'.

1. **Analytical** – what is the gap in expectation/results? What's the unmet need in them or in you? Analysing the gap(s) accurately gives you real insight as to the way forward.

2. **Assertive** (not aggressive) – match the other person's level of authority and support with warmth of approach.

3. **Aware** – that you and others have emotional triggers. Pressing them can be fraught with danger, especially if resolution is what you're aiming for.

4. **Courageous** – it's a difference of opinion. Be bold enough to hear others out and strong enough to hold out for what you believe. Stepping up to challenging friends and long-standing colleagues can be difficult. This is a good time to be courageous.

5. **Calm** – if you can stay composed, your brain will function better and you'll be able think, you'll be able to make sense of the conversation and keep it rational.

6. **Curious** – if you can take an inquiring, probing, investigating, attentive approach, it helps you avoid getting emotionally drawn into the 'battle' of the conflict. When we get sucked into the battle, lines get drawn up swiftly; we become defensive, closed to any solutions other than our own. Stay curious because it helps you be more objective.

7. **Clever** – sometimes you're right; sometimes others are right. Clever people are able to cut through the fluff, see the point and appreciate that others have different and sometimes richer/better perspectives than they do. Be gracious when you're clever enough to see it.

8. **Decisive** – when it's time to act, time to decide, do it. Make your decision and stick to it. Do everything you can to make it work. PDCA. Act quickly even if it's not pleasant.

9. **Fair** – show due diligence as you evaluate the situation and propose a solution or consider their proposal. Remember, what goes around comes around.

10. **Firm** – when the issue is non-negotiable. Great negotiators know exactly what their 'walk away' is. As a manager, you may be asked to present changes or decisions that are non-negotiable. Present them as such. Leave no room for hope where none exists – this ultimately helps to manage expectations more effectively.

11. **Gracious** – challenge the behaviour, the problem, the issue, not the person. Civility can go out the door when tempers rise; positions become entrenched during arguments. Kindness and diplomacy can go a long way to helping resolve conflicts, especially when backed up with a little gracious fierceness. (Don't you love that term – gracious fierceness?)

12. **Honest** – in the face of conflict, honesty can get stretched to breaking point. Being able to express yourself frankly without being rude or hurtful is a great skill to learn. Examine the 'rights and wrongs' as objectively as you can. Acknowledge the danger of ignoring conflict issues especially between people; otherwise resentment can fester and do terrible damage.

13. **Impartial** – staying appropriately detached from issues that don't involve you can help you avoid getting drawn into the Drama Triangle (Kaufmann). There's a time to keep out of the argument and help them handle the issue themselves.

14. **Pragmatic** – commit to reaching a resolution and ask for their commitment. There's a time to negotiate, barter, fight for your cause. There's a time to be realistic, practical and logical.

15. **Prepared** – do your homework and be ready. Delay if necessary/possible. Collect facts, evidence, stats, insights. Avoid relying on rumour, insinuation or gossip.

16. **Sensible** – they may have a point. It may be that you are wrong or partially incorrect. In maintaining objectivity and avoiding escalation you can be big enough to 'see sense' when it hits you in the face and gracious enough to admit it.

17. **Visionary** – be crystal clear about the ultimate goal; when push comes to shove, what's most important in the context of the conflict/disagreement? What are you aiming for and why?

18. **Well-informed** – have the facts and evidence in order. Know where the gaps are. Consider external influencers as well as immediate factors.

19. **Willing to call a 'time out'** – when tempers are frayed; emotions are high; there's a need to reflect; cool down; establish facts (rather than hearsay).

20. **Willing to negotiate/change your mind** – this is a real sign of maturity and reason if, when faced with a case or evidence that is strong and just, you demonstrate behavioural flexibility. It's not just a woman's prerogative to change her mind. Men can do it too.

In essence

- Using the term courageous conversation or constructive dialogue will be more helpful than referring to them as 'difficult' since that reinforces the negative and will likely increase stress levels

- Constructive dialogues are two-way conversations, not monologues held by the leader-manager

- These conversations are all about getting results while maintaining good working relationships

- The guided pathway gives you a practical step-by-step process to help you prepare, conduct, control and later review the conversations

- Use the checklist to set the dialogue up for mutual success

CHAPTER 10

Effectiveness – Getting it in the muscle

Plan, rehearse, practice

'Practice is the act of rehearsing a behaviour over and over ... with the aim of improving or mastering it.' - Unknown

Managers I meet know a great deal about managing and leading. After all, they have the experience of being managed and led, which is a great start. They've all managed projects, tasks, challenges in their work and personal lives so they have those insights too. They've watched people they respect, and some they don't, manage situations and people.

They have knowledge. That's the 'what'. They know they need to plan, organise, decide, communicate, allocate responsibilities, motivate, discipline, negotiate, develop, influence, delegate, monitor and review. Yet they weren't born with these skills. They developed and honed the skills over time.

You're a manager. You're good at lots of different things. Think of one skill you are particularly proud of having. So how did you get good at it? Did you do it once and it was perfect? Or did you need to repeat and practice? Chances are you rehearsed; you reviewed what you did well; saw what needed to improve; you improved and repeated.

> 'In theory there's no difference between theory and practice. In practice, there is.' – Yogi Berra

When I coach an individual manager or facilitate groups of leader-managers, they invariably have a number of prioritised actions to take back to the business; to do something differently; to practice a skill; to rehearse before delivering. It's part of our deal.

This requires them to stop doing the thing they've been doing that isn't working any longer, and start doing something else. I say start, because invariably, when we start to form a new skill or habit, it isn't perfected at first attempt. We repeat the practice; we rehearse to improve the practice – and the more frequently the better. Continuous improvement (Kaizen) is the goal.

The science of successful learning tells us the three criteria for 'getting it in the muscle' are:

1. correct repetition

2. rehearsal and

3. frequency

OPDCA – Practice and refine cycle

When I worked with Toyota I learned a great deal about Deming's PDCA process. It's a well-known 'cycle of improvement and effectiveness'. This is a great frame for getting it in the muscle, because practice, rehearsal and performance review are an integral part of the process.

In true continuous improvement fashion, someone has now added 'O' – which stands for Observe the current situation – to Deming's PDCA and I offer it here and you can make up your own mind about its value.

Observe – what's happening in the current situation

Plan – having identified root cause, set targets, plan countermeasures

Do – practice to achieve standard, apply action, monitor action against target

Check – progress, what works, what needs to change, refine

Adjust and adapt to changing circumstances; to improve where necessary and repeat what's successful.

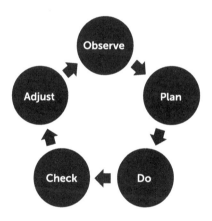

Fig. 35 OPDCA

Permission to be a learner (and not be perfect just yet)

There's an attitude prevalent in organisations (and in life) that because you've 'learned' or, more accurately, 'been taught or shown' a new skill, technique or tool, that you should know it and be able to use it … effortlessly, and if you can't, it's because the tool or technique isn't worthwhile.

Michelin star chefs don't become so by learning something and just doing it once or twice The great golfers, rugby players and tennis players don't win championships year after year just by turning up; Willie Walsh hasn't run BA successfully for years by not learning new things and trying new approaches. Same goes for Richard Branson of Virgin, who is constantly trying new things, pushing the boundaries of science, service, technology and finance. The truth is, being truly good at something takes trial and error, rehearsal, practice, checking, refining and repeating. It takes commitment.

> Being truly good at something takes trial and error, rehearsal, practice, checking, refining and repeating. It takes commitment.

As you know, there are different ways to learn. We all learn via some combination of theory, practice, analysing and trying out new ideas. Do you like to sit, read and reflect? Do you like to question and scrutinise? Do you prefer to check out the rules, read the manual or procedures first? Do you like to jump straight into action and think later? If you wish to research this further, check out Honey and Mumford's Learning Styles online.

Once you establish your 'styles' you can test how they work for you. Remember, others in your team may learn in a similar way or in a different way from you. It's not about right and wrong, it's about appreciating how best to help people learn so that they can perform well at work and fulfil their potential. If you're an activist and work with reflectors, it will help you and them, if they have time to review and consider before they give an opinion or suggest action. Find a way to work with your and others' learning styles, not against them.

When I was at boarding school, I used to think my piano teacher was a demanding and relentless woman. Nothing but getting it right would do. She wanted me to be a really good piano player. To this end she'd constantly critique and criticise my playing. When I repeated the same mistakes in notes or timings, she would stop me, show me how to do it right, then get me to repeat that short piece over and over, till I didn't have to think about it any longer. Then we'd move on to the next section. She used to say, 'Let's get it in the muscle, Catherine'; 'Practice makes perfect, Catherine!'; 'You're making mistakes because it's not in the muscle.' It wasn't easy for me to achieve the high standard she set me. It took time and massive effort and a level of self-discipline I didn't have much of then, but when it all came together it was worth it in the end. Her incantations stay with me to this day.

The three learning gifts of a Leader-Manager

1. The greatest 'learning' gift you can give someone who needs to learn something new is **permission to be a learner**. This means not necessarily 'getting it' immediately (some people need to think about it and reflect on how it makes sense to them; others need to know the underlying theory, so it has context and rigour; yet others – the pragmatists – just need to 'try it out' and see what happens; and the activists just want to stop talking about it and get it done.

2. The second 'learning' gift you can bring others is to **use OPDCA** in your practice, be a role model for it in order that they see, feel and experience it. Using it consistently will educate them in the practice, enable them to develop the practice and encourage them by using it successfully. This is real leadership. Being a role model for rigour and process.

3. The third 'learning' gift you can give is that of **accountability**. When you or members of your team learn something new, whether by accident or design, get them into the habit of sharing it with others. In one organisation I work with, teams and small groups get together regularly (at least weekly) for 20 minutes and have 'Toolbox Talks'. These can take the form of 'sharing what I learned'; 'sharing what went wrong and how we solved it'; 'sharing how I solved it'; 'sharing what we did that got it right' and 'sharing how to do it'. It's a peer-learning situation; no fancy PowerPoint;

no fancy materials. Just a whiteboard, enthusiasm and willingness to share successes, ideas, failures and learning with others to make the team and organisation a better one for all.

The expert in anything was once a beginner.

The Forgetting Curve

'I hear and I forget. I see and I remember. I do and I understand.' – Confucius

In order to be effective you have to know what good looks like. Knowing 'what' to do is essential for managers' day-to-day survival. Knowing 'how' is given much less emphasis, unless things are going wrong or you're working for an organisation that is committed to developing its leaders. Knowing 'why' is the most common missing element in being effective. Clarity of purpose is the 'why'.

One way or another, managers learn what they need to do and most get on and do the best job they can. The lucky ones are supported by attending management and development programmes, by having a coach or a mentor to help them grow and improve this aspect of their role. However, there's some interesting research on what helps us remember what we've learned and on just how easy it is to forget massive amounts of what we've been told.

Ebbinghaus's research indicated that total recall (100%) for him was achieved only at the time of acquisition and that the greatest amount of 'forgetting' occurred soon after learning. Following that, retention dropped away very quickly:

- 20 minutes later 42% of the memorised list was lost

- 24 hours later 67% of what he learned had vanished

- one month later 79% had been forgotten, meaning just 21% was retained.

Even if you learn something well, you can forget it. Without rehearsal, we forget things over time, or we lose the detail and it's easy to lose confidence as our skills deteriorate. I speak French, yet each time we visit France, my French is rusty, hesitant; I search my memory for words and phrases. My comprehension remains at a good standard, but it takes me a week or so to get back into speaking fluently and confidently. I aim to add to my vocabulary and improve my expression each time, yet each time I leave France, my competence takes a dive and I have to work at recapturing my former level before I can begin to make improvements. It's an iterative process.

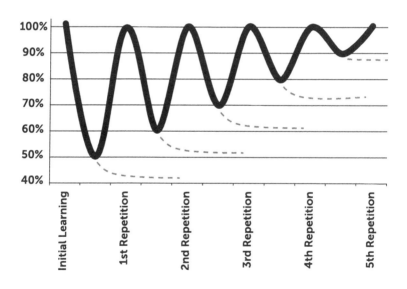

Fig. 36 The Forgetting Curve

In order to get it in the muscle, you must rehearse, rehearse, rehearse; then practice, practice, practice before you get to the stage when it will come automatically, intuitively.

If you want to remember helpful tools and techniques, stepped processes, it's important to revisit, review and revise until you can recall it at will, and at this stage you'll be able to teach others too.

Put into development terms, it simply means that each revisit of learned material reinforces its retention.

Memory is a combination of three stages or processes:

1. Acquire (learn)

2. Store (encode)

3. Remember (retrieve) information.

What leader-manager skills do you want to 'get in the muscle'?

Knowing is not the same as doing

'To know and not to do is not to know.' – Stephen Covey, Author, *7 Habits of Highly Effective People*

In the last section you've read about how 'not to forget'… or put another way, how to improve retention. At the same time, having the knowledge is not the same as using the knowledge. The map is not the territory. For example, most people know they need to face up and deal with difficult people or difficult situations but it doesn't mean they 'do it' – or indeed that they know 'how to do it well'.

One of the most consistent areas L-Ms tell me they find challenging is having difficult conversations with others – whether their boss, their direct reports, other stakeholders, clients, suppliers, etc. This isn't just a core skill L-Ms need. I'd go so far as to say it's a life skill. Knowing you need to have a difficult conversation is one thing. It's another knowing 'how to do it', because you have a plan and you have prepared. Finally, it's about having the confidence or courage to 'do it then reviewing it when it's over.

Story: Matt is a technically experienced and qualified operational manager in the construction industry. With 22 years' of service, his current project was due to complete in the next three months and he was uncertain about 'what next?' and 'where next?'. He had been meaning to speak to his boss about it but just never got around to it.

Matt, however, was becoming increasingly anxious and the uncertainty was beginning to affect his family situation. But he was anxious about doing what he knew he needed to do – have a robust conversation with his boss about the future. Matt felt so powerless at times that in his own mind he thought he might resign from his job. The less action he took the more anxious he became. He made excuses for not speaking to his boss – 'He's always soooo busy with other stuff'.

In this situation, Matt knew he needed to find the courage, assertiveness, drive (or whatever it was that he was lacking) and to take action; to speak to his boss. Sometimes when we know we need to do something and we don't, it's a good idea to challenge ourselves with a simple question:

Do we really want to do it? If yes, the proof will be the action we take. If there's no action, there's no proof and our resistance is greater than our will.

> 'The definition of insanity is doing the same thing over and over again, but expecting different results.' – Albert Einstein

Getting it in the muscle

In the process of learning something new we go through what's known as the learning through practice process. When our skills are honed to the extent that they are second nature, they are what I refer to as being 'in the muscle'.

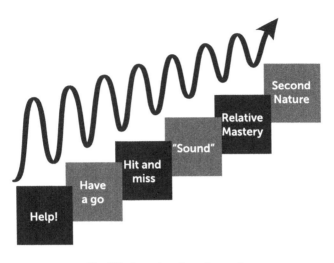

Fig 37 Learning through practice

Here's the typical pathway to success:

'Help!' – you're a beginner – relatively clueless, often optimistic; learning the ropes, still not fully aware of just how much you don't know and how much you need to learn. In the Cycle of Competence, this is the Unconscious Incompetence stage (you don't know what you don't know).

'Have a go' – you're a novice – learning basic skills and approaches, confidence growing, often a level of naivety about what you know or how much you know.

'Hit and miss' – you're a realist, more aware of what you know, what you don't and the gap. Beginning to notice a few successes and identifying areas of difficulty and challenge (gap in performance). May be a level of discouragement as you find out just how much you don't know or that you find out just how difficult 'good' is to achieve. In the Cycle of Competence, this is the Conscious Incompetence stage (beginning to realise what you don't know).

'Sound' – more hit than miss. More consistent in your approach but now, when it doesn't work, you know why and have ideas about how to get it better next time. Less defeated. More determined. More confident.

'Nearly there' – it's coming a little more automatically now. Getting to understand the nuances of each technique; understanding the situational contexts that influence performance (weather, ground conditions, etc). In the Cycle of Competence, this is the Conscious Competence stage.

'Second nature' – you know when you've achieved this when you look back and notice you did it without even thinking … and you got it right; it went to plan. Another example is when someone else says 'How do you do that?' and you're no longer really sure of the actual steps you took. This is a sign you're performing at a level of 'unconscious competence'. This is the sign you've 'got it in the muscle'; it's an automatic reaction. In the Cycle of Competence, this is the Unconscious Competence stage.

> When our skills are honed to the extent that they are second nature, they are 'in the muscle'.

At the same time as you are learning through practice, you are going through four stages called the Cycle of Competence

The Cycle of Competence: four stages

1. Unconscious incompetence (don't know what you don't know)

2. Conscious incompetence (know you don't know)

3. Conscious competence (aware of your level of skill/learning)

4. Unconscious competence (no need to make a conscious effort – it's second nature).

Story of Chris – Getting it in the muscle through practice
Chris had been working in this company for about 18 months. She loved the job, she knew there was a contribution she could make towards getting the projects completed more effectively; she was keen to improve others' understanding of the impact of their decisions. She enjoyed working with her colleagues and yet she was seriously contemplating leaving a job she loved in a business she wanted to continue working in.

Unconscious Incompetence

Each week, she met with other regional managers, some peers and some more senior to her. They didn't listen to her; they interrupted her when she spoke; when someone else repeated a point she'd made, they would be acknowledged; they weren't open to doing things differently even when she showed them proof of effectiveness and cost savings.

Conscious Incompetence

She noticed how stressed she was becoming just thinking about the meeting. She got into the habit of second guessing what objections others in the meeting might raise to the points she suggested or strategies she needed them to buy into. After some months she was thinking of the meeting as 'a weekly battleground'. She tried all sorts of things – bringing more data, writing longer and more detailed reports, etc. Their offhand attitude towards her made her angry.

Over the months her frustration showed; she competed with them by shouting them down; by arguing her point; by ignoring what they said. 'It was either that or not bother to say anything – even when I know more about my area of expertise than they ever will,' she told me. Nothing she was doing was having the desired effect and she was at a loss to know what to do. She was enraged when they made (what she called 'bloody minded') avoidable poor-quality decisions. She realised she just did not know what to do or how to change their approach to her.

You'll no doubt have experienced something like this at some stage and it's a real challenge to face down and overcome aggressive and competitive behaviours that can become ingrained and repetitive.

Without meaning to she fell into the 'if you can't beat them join them' trap.

Conscious Competence

Chris was at the stage where she had lots of good skills and awareness; she was aware of what was and wasn't working; she told me she had tried lots of different approaches and none of them were working. She was conscious of putting so much energy into changing them, that she was exhausted and feeling like a failure. She was therefore thinking of leaving the organisation.

When we met she had all but given up. She had drafted her resignation letter. 'I don't want to leave but I feel I must if I can't get them to change.'

What she needed was to step back from 'being in the meeting' to reflect on 'what was going on in the meeting'. We set to work on four areas:

- giving her a new take and insight into what was going on in the dynamics of that regional meeting

- developing different thinking around her role in and out of the meeting

- revisiting and clarifying the scope of her responsibilities; where they started and ended and in relation to others'

- planning and practising different strategies to give her options to choose from when dealing with behaviours that cropped up.

Chris learned a number of specific techniques and approaches; we looked at language; phraseology; timing of suggestions, recommendations, etc. She practised these techniques elsewhere first. She became more fluent using them and her confidence grew.

The meetings continued to be difficult but she learned to notice earlier and earlier, when her stress levels were rising – and how to stop them from escalating. She practised staying calm; slowing down her speech; speaking more quietly and leaving occasional silences before she continued. These approaches helped her 'stay in control'; stay rational and unemotional, when others started behaving aggressively. She learned how and when to detach herself and 'how to fight my battles' in the meeting.

> 'The more I practice the luckier I get.'
> – Arnold Palmer, Champion Golfer

Unconscious Competence

About three or four months after Chris had started putting the various strategies and techniques into practice, one of the regional managers pulled her aside at the end of the meeting and said, 'We missed you for the past two meetings – we all ended up rowing again, like we did in the past. It was only when I noticed you weren't with us that I realised you help us all stay calm and discuss the issues without all the arguments.'

When this happened, Chris realised that taking a different thinking approach to the meetings and changing her behaviour, practising the techniques until she didn't need to 'think about them any more' was working – for her and for others. She finally learned that when she changed, others changed. She led the change.

> I'm not telling you it is going to be easy;
> I'm telling you it's going to be worth it.

Continuous improvement and advancement

Once you have the basics in place and they come automatically, you begin the process again but at a different level of performance.

Stepping up to the next level of complexity or advancement, you repeat the process at each level, until each is second nature, then you advance again.

One of the traps you want to avoid is jumping ahead or advancing too quickly. Calibrating the level of the 'jump' is a skill in itself. It can be too easy, too difficult or just right. Setting yourself levels of complexity or advancement where the gap is too much is likely to lead to failure and disappointment. Too easy can lead to complacency and ultimately a reduction in confidence.

The Payoffs for being a willing lifelong learner:

What do you get from putting in the effort?

- A great sense of achievement
- Greater output. The brain is a muscle to be exercised – so use it or lose it (See John's Story below)
- Being a role model to others in the team – peers, colleagues, and direct reports
- Capability to handle situations more effectively – this can have benefits for you, your department, your project, your organisation
- Flexibility – the more you know, the more skills you have in your tool kit, the better for you and any situation you face. It gives you options and choices and enables you to adapt your approach to a wider number and complexity of people, issues and contexts
- Lead by example: demonstrate commitment, self-awareness and honesty
- Takes issues away or resolves them more easily/quickly
- Avoid stagnation
- Other people notice you are open to learning and make the effort – your reputation can be enhanced, leading to greater

opportunities to contribute and succeed

- Impact under pressure – more resourceful, better presence of mind.

John's Story: My father John was the best role model I've ever met for lifelong learning. At the age of 35 he taught himself about architecture so that he could redesign his business premises; at the age of 52, quite by accident of circumstance, he learned how to paint landscapes using oil and watercolour. He became a well-known and in-demand artist over the next twenty years.

At the age of 65 he bought his first PC, leaned how to use Microsoft Word. Soon he began writing his first book – about a man who had lived in our home, General Thomas Cloney, leader of the 1798 rebellion. After publication, John was invited to give talks at the local and regional historical societies and, unexpectedly, he became a local celebrity.

Twenty years later, he became seriously interested in technology; he bought a mobile phone and asked a nephew to teach him abbreviated texting (eg tnx, lol, CUl8r, etc). Soon after he acquired a laptop so he could have Wi-Fi access wherever he went; then he downloaded Skype so he could see and speak to his children in other countries. He discovered Wikipedia. Appalled about inaccuracies he found there, he checked out how to make additions and revisions and he spent months updating information on local history and the town he lived in.

Finally, about a year before he died at the age of 95, he discovered YouTube. He loved it and would search for topics he knew little about and would regale us with stories of what he'd found. I am convinced that his willingness to keep learning, his incessant curiosity about the world and his determination to keep up with new developments meant he was using his brain – and this was one of the secrets to his long, happy and fulfilled life.

This might well have been his advice:

> 'Don't lower your expectations to meet your performance. Raise your level of performance to meet your expectations. Expect the best of yourself and then do what is necessary to make it a reality.'
> – Ralph Marston

In essence

- If you want to be good at something you must be open to learning about it

- Mastery or competence requires the willingness to practice, repeat, apply and to make improvements over time

- The OPDCA is a robust cycle for success

- Give yourself and others permission to be learners and do not expect instant mastery

- Accountability can be encouraged by getting members of your team to share their skills by teaching others

- The Forgetting Curve is easily forgotten. Retention of knowledge and skills takes practice and repetition

- People move through four levels of competence before something becomes 'second nature'.

Final Thoughts

Once you master the skills set out in this book you can be proud of yourself. You will have a range of approaches and tools at your disposal that will increase your confidence and give you the assurance you deserve.

Using your understanding of the three generations at work will enable you to take a more considered approach to your team and colleagues. These insights can stretch your thinking and help you adapt your behaviour in such a way that you and the business get more from the individuals concerned.

Given the hectic nature of the world around us, taking time out to think and plan before acting may well feel like a luxury. If it is (and I don't believe it is), it is one luxury you must allow yourself. Truly, it is a necessary habit which, if you adopt it, will serve you well.

None of us are born with the skills to lead and manage; they develop in us over time. Whether you start in the playground, at college or once you start work, it takes effort, intention, practice, rehearsal and review to really hone the skills and to become agile and flexible. Each chapter in the book is there to get you thinking, to give you insights, ideas about 'why', 'what' and 'how'.

It's easy to do the easy part of being a manager. What's needed is resourceful, agile and flexible people who can manage difficult conversations well, who have enough understanding about resistance to change, not only not to make it worse but to be able to create a climate of change-acceptance. In managing performance, being self-disciplined about planning and preparation and being resilient in the face of everyday challenges, you have a chance to show your true colours, your true potential.

The road to success as a leader-manager today is as exciting as it's ever been … perhaps even more so. It's full of challenge and opportunity for those willing to lead, for those willing to do what's needed to generate engagement, to find a way to retain talent and to continue to grow as a person and as a manager. Organisations need great leader-managers at all levels.

There has never been a better time to learn about, practice and become a leader-manager. I hope you will keep this book handy; use it to help you learn; share the contents with others and enjoy your voyage of exploration.

The stage is set, your audience awaits you.

Author Biography

People love Catherine's Irish accent and often say to her, 'I wish I could tape you, so I can keep you in my head, giving me sound advice and encouragement and making me think.'

Catherine has been in and around managers and leaders all her life. She grew up within a vibrant family business in Southern Ireland and started her career in business management. She studied at Shannon College of Hotel Management but soon left hotels and joined Shell UK. After 12 years in learning and development and line management in Shell she founded BlueQuay Limited in 2005.

Catherine is a highly experienced, qualified consultant, facilitator and executive coach with over 20 years' experience in corporate life. She specialises in helping develop leaders and managers in such a way that they can significantly increase their confidence, competence and impact in the organisations that employ them. She has extensive experience with intact and virtual teams, coaching directors and senior managers in a range of industries. Working with blue chip companies in the areas of leadership, change and management development, she especially enjoys working with individuals, teams and large groups who are in the process of business change and those who want to grow and develop their leader-managers.

She has worked in a number of London consultancies and for seven years ran an L&D consultancy called Making Connections. She has also worked for several years as an operations director in the UK voluntary sector.

Together with a strong business-minded approach, her warm, encouraging yet challenging style helps people to build their confidence and skills, to work more effectively and to become more focused about their future plans and contributions.

A Chartered Fellow of the Chartered Institute of Personnel and Development (FCIPD) she is also a Fellow of the Chartered Management Institute (FCMI) and a Member of the Association for Coaching (MAC). She is a graduate of the Collaborative Leaders Programme and a qualified BS11000 Collaborative Leadership facilitator (MICW). Catherine is a professionally qualified coach and has a Diploma in Corporate Coaching. She is also a trained coaching supervisor.

Previous and recent clients include:

Sector	Client
Civil Engineering and Construction	BAM Nuttall, John Sisk & Son, Mace
FMCG/Retail	Diageo, Euromaster, Guinness, ATS Euromaster
IT	Oracle, Fujitsu
Motor/Manufacturers	Lexus, Toyota, Jemca, Vauxhall Motors
Oil and Gas	Shell, Eon E&P
Media Tech	EE, NBC Universal
Utilities	RWE (UK Headquarters), npower (Retail Division)

Contact Catherine via email: cjoyce@blue-quay.co.uk – she would love to hear from you.

Lightning Source UK Ltd.
Milton Keynes UK
UKOW06f1831140216

268347UK00001B/2/P